FROM GRIEF TO GLORY

FROM GRIEF TO GLORY

SPIRITUAL JOURNEYS OF MOURNING PARENTS

❦

James W. Bruce III

THE BANNER OF TRUTH TRUST

THE BANNER OF TRUTH TRUST
3 Murrayfield Road, Edinburgh EH12 6EL, UK
P.O. Box 621, Carlisle, PA 17013, USA

*

First published by Crossway Books 2002
First Banner of Truth edition 2008
© James W. Bruce III 2008

ISBN-13: 978 0 85151 996 8

*

Typeset in 10.5/14 pt Sabon Oldstyle at
The Banner of Truth Trust, Edinburgh

Printed in the USA by
Versa Press, Inc.
Peoria, IL

To Him
who took children in His arms,
laid His hands on them,
and blessed them.

❦

In Memory of
John Cameron Bruce
(January 20, 1997 – March 16, 1997)

Our son was with us for fifty-five days, and then . . .
'he was not; for God took him.'

CONTENTS

PART THREE: THE PATH TO GLORY

Preface to the
New Edition

The Bruce clan motto is 'Fuimus', a Latin word that means 'We have been.' My son, John Cameron Bruce, has been, and he has left his mark—on me, my family and others who have been touched by his life. His work is over, but ours is not; so, we in turn must seek to leave our own marks for the glory of God and the welfare of those we meet along the way. May it be said of us when we leave this earthly life for our heavenly home that we 'have done what we could'.

I am thankful for the many individuals who, over the years, have told me how this book has ministered to them during very difficult times, and I am grateful to the Banner of Truth Trust for keeping it in publication. I continue to pray that our great and sovereign Lord will use this small offering to comfort and strengthen families as they 'travel on' and walk the path that leads from grief to glory.

This is my comfort in my affliction, that your promise gives me life. (Psa. 119:50)

James W. Bruce, III
June, 2008

FOREWORD

This is truly a remarkable book. Since reading it, I have often wished it had been available when I was pastoring a congregation. It is the very book I would have wanted to put into the hands of grieving parents.

My friend Jay Bruce has written out of the deep pain Joni, his wife, and he suffered when their little boy died after only fifty-five days in this world. The book is not just an account of their pilgrimage at that harrowing time. It is also a fascinating compendium of the experience of men and women whose names are familiar even to some non-Christians—Calvin, Luther, Bunyan, Charles Wesley. These people all experienced the same tribulation and have set down their inmost thoughts and expressed their heartache.

The book would be significant for this unique collection of quotations alone. But the spiritual insight and godly grace with which Jay Bruce writes make this volume a real treasure to own and a particular blessing to read.

ERIC J. ALEXANDER
Retired Pastor,
St George's Tron Church,
Glasgow, Scotland

He was the music of our home,
　　A day that knew no night.
The fragrance of our garden bower,
　　A thing all smiles and light.

Above the couch we bent and prayed
　　In the half-lighted room,
As the bright hues of infant life
　　Sank slowly into gloom.

The form remained; but there was now
　　No soul our love to share;
Farewell, with weeping hearts, we said,
　　Child of our love and care.

But years are moving quickly past,
　　And time will soon be o'er;
Death shall be swallowed up in life
　　On the immortal shore.

Then shall we clasp that hand once more,
　　And smooth that golden hair;
Then shall we kiss those lips again,
　　When we shall meet him there.[1]

HORATIUS BONAR

[1] Horatius Bonar, *The Christian Hymn Book for the Sanctuary and Home* (Dayton, Ohio: Christian Publishing Association, 1875). Bonar was a nineteenth-century Scottish minister and hymn writer. He and his wife lost five children in successive bereavements.

THIS IS MY SON,
WHOM GOD HAS GIVEN ME IN THIS PLACE

Behold, 'children are a gift of the Lord.' So the psalmist says. And, 'children's children are the crown of old men.' Indeed, in Psalm 127 the Bible proclaims that children are a reward. 'Like arrows in the hand of a warrior, so are the children of one's youth. Happy is the man who has his quiver full of them.'

Few things match the joy that children bring to a family. Even fewer things rival the sorrow of a family that buries a child. My family has known both. We have been twice blessed by the birth of a child, once grieved by the death of a son. We have also known the sorrows of a miscarriage and the celebration of adopting and bringing home a baby boy.

On a Sunday evening in March of 1997, my wife and I walked through the darkest trial of our faith—the death of our beloved infant son, John Cameron Bruce. But in the midst of the grief attending our son's illness and death, we always trusted that God was yet at work, watching over and comforting us by his Spirit, with his Word and through his church, ordaining all things for his glory and our good, and for the good of our son, too.

John Cameron was born on a sunny winter afternoon. He was a fine-looking lad, but the Lord knitted him together and formed his inward parts with a genetic kidney disorder. The most critical complication of the disease involved his lungs, which never developed sufficiently to sustain his life apart from a ventilator.

During the next few weeks, I kept a journal and chronicled the course of my son's life. Most entries I made at night as I reflected on the day's events, which always included some time by John Cameron's bed. I liked to visit him late at night. As Florence Nightingale said: 'Life is a hard fight, a struggle, a wrestling with the principle of evil, hand to hand, foot to foot. Every inch of the way is disputed. But the night is given us to take breath and to pray, to drink deep at the fountain of power. The day, to use the strength that has been given us, to go forth to work with it till the evening.'[1]

That is what the nights were like for me when the hospital room lights were dimmed, other visitors were few, and the nurses seemed to go about their work quietly, as quietly as a parent might move about a child's bedroom at night so as not to disturb his sleep. I appreciated those times. They were refreshing and helped to ease my anxiety. The quiet, confident voice of a nurse has a calming effect.

---

[1] Edythe Draper, *Quotations for the Christian World* (Wheaton, IL: Tyndale House Publishers, 1992).

I share a few of my journal entries now as a brief look at the ups and downs of John Cameron's life and that of a father whose son is dying.

❦

Tuesday, January 21, 1997. Yesterday at 3:21 P.M. our son, John Cameron, was born. From birth he has been in intensive care, with complications affecting his lungs, heart, and kidneys. I pray, O Lord, that you would be merciful unto him. We look to you alone to raise him up. And how thankful I am that you hear the prayers and supplications of your saints on his and our behalf. Hear, O Lord, from heaven; hear and save. *Soli Deo Gloria*—Glory to God alone!

Wednesday, January 22. The prayers of the saints ascend for John Cameron in more numbers than we know, and the Lord has heard and provided mercies sufficient for the day. John has shown a measure of improvement, and I continue to commend him to our Lord's keeping. We look to you, Lord, in all matters concerning his life and health and eternal happiness.

Saturday, March 8. John Cameron's left lung collapsed, but the doctors were able to save him by inserting a chest tube.

Tuesday, March 11. The past few days have been quite a blessing. Good friends have come to comfort and encourage us . . . This afternoon the doctors again said that it appeared we are losing the battle for John Cameron; they suggested removing one of his kidneys (in the hope that a lung might be able to expand). At 6:30 P.M. we met for prayer. At 7:02 the surgeon began the operation, which was completed at approximately 8:15. John Cameron survived the surgery. Perhaps this will be the means God has appointed for John's recovery. Lord, may it be so. Amen.

Sunday, March 23. John Cameron died on Sunday, March 16, at 9:21 in the evening. He died in the arms of his mother and father; our last act as parents was to commend him (and ourselves) to Christ and his good keeping. John's death is one of the most profound experiences of my life, for we wrestled with things of an eternal nature. All during his life I prayed that God would either grant him life and health or spare us from the difficult decisions. But God did neither.

❧

Our son was with us for fifty-five days, and then, in the language of Scripture, 'he was not; for God took him' (*Gen.* 5:24). We fought the good fight for nearly two months in the hospital's Neonatal Intensive Care Unit, trying heroic medical measures. But the battle was not for us to win or lose, for Christ alone holds the keys of life and death, and he shares those keys with no-one. The duty to fight was ours; the outcome belonged to God.

As the days passed without much success from the medical treatments, I began to sense that John Cameron might not survive. I thought his death would be easier for us if we were not there and simply received a call in the night from his doctors. I dreaded the thought of being by my son's side as he died. I did not know if I could bear to watch him close his eyes in death. Receiving the bad news would be difficult enough. But watching it unfold before my very eyes—I groaned at the prospect. 'Have mercy, O Lord. Spare my son', I prayed, 'that I might not have sorrow upon sorrow.'

But God's ways are not our ways, and he would not let me play the coward or escape the cords of death so easily. What I feared most came to pass, and (now I can say) we had the blessing of being with our son the night he died. As his earthly life ebbed away, we prayed for him and commended him to Christ, the Good Shepherd, who alone is able to shepherd beyond the grave. Our last act as his parents was to embrace him as he died.

The Lord had set the number of John Cameron's days; in his book they were written, every one of them (*Psa.* 139:16; *Job* 14:5). God had beheld his unformed substance and decreed the bounds beyond which he could not pass—fifty-five days and no more. Then, when he had accomplished his good purpose, the end came quietly and peacefully.

Until that day came, it was as if we had crossed a ford and, like Jacob of old, had been wrestling with God.

But on the Sunday night that John Cameron died, God touched our thigh and put it out of joint. We wrestled no more and sought only a blessing from him for the son we loved so much and for ourselves.

Since that time, my wife and I have had many occasions to tell others of God's sovereign grace and the paradox of joy in the midst of suffering. 'Let me learn by paradox', goes the prayer:

> *that the way down is the way up,*
> *that to be low is to be high,*
> *that the broken heart is the healed heart,*
> *that to have nothing is to possess all,*
> *that to bear the cross is to wear the crown,*
> *that the valley is the place of vision.*
> *Let me find Thy light in my darkness,*
> *Thy life in my death, Thy joy in my sorrow,*
> *Thy glory in my valley.*[2]

We have also learned a measure of the truth expressed by the apostle Paul to the Corinthian church: 'Blessed be the God and Father of our Lord Jesus Christ, the Father of mercies and God of all comfort, who comforts us in all our tribulation, that we may be able to comfort those who are in any trouble, with the comfort with which we ourselves are comforted by God' (2 *Cor.* 1:3-4). These truths, as John Bunyan said, 'have been burnt into my heart as with a hot iron.'

---

[2] Arthur Bennett, ed., *The Valley of Vision, A Collection of Puritan Prayers and Devotions* (Edinburgh: Banner of Truth, 1975).

Looking back on the death of my son, I see now the value of trudging through life's struggles with others who have trod the same path. 'The soldier falters alone; but, in fellowship with his comrades, he advances with confidence.' As true as this is on the battlefield, so is it in times of grief. Scripture proclaims this truth. 'Two are better than one', says Solomon, 'because they have a good reward for their labour. For if they fall, one will lift up his companion' (*Eccles.* 4:9-10).

Such camaraderie may exist though time or great distance separates the soldiers, for this fellowship arises out of the shared experience. Mark the words of the great English reformer Hugh Latimer who, shortly before being martyred for his faith in 1555, sent a farewell letter to fellow sufferers in which he wrote, 'Set before you that though the weather is stormy and foul, yet you do not go alone; many others pass by the same path; their company might cause you to be the more courageous and cheerful.'

No doubt Latimer greatly helped those faithful Englishmen who followed him into the flames for the cause of Christ. But who has set us a Christian example of how to bear up under the loss of a child? Today with advances in medical technology and the aid of skillful physicians, we seldom know firsthand of a child dying. (Yet, as my wife and I have learned, this is a far more common thing than most people realize.) So let us look to times past when losing a child at a tender age was perhaps the rule, not the exception. Let us look to an age when one could say,

'Death is a near neighbour, and one death in a family is but the forerunner and warning of another.'

The list of great men and women of the Christian church who shed tears over a departed child or grandchild is a long one: John Calvin wept for his infant son; Martin Luther for a daughter; John Bunyan also for a daughter. George Whitefield buried a son, as did George Müller. Charles Wesley lost five of his eight children. Horatius Bonar parted with five children in successive bereavements. Charles Haddon Spurgeon mourned a grandson. Some of their names may be unfamiliar, but they all passed along the same path and climbed the same difficult hill. Their company may make us cheerful and brave. Their strength may become ours.

We who have lost the company of a child do not go alone. We may keep company with these men and their wives as we pass through the Valley of Baca—the Valley of Weeping spoken of in Psalm 84:5–7: 'Blessed are those whose strength is in you, in whose heart are the highways to Zion. As they go through the Valley of Baca they make it a place of springs; the early rain also covers it with pools. They go from strength to strength; each one appears before God in Zion" (ESV).

The comfort obtained by others', wrote C. H. Spurgeon, 'may often prove helpful to another, just as wells would be used by those who come after. We read some good book full of consolation. Ah! we think our brother has been there before us and dug this well for us as well as for himself. Travellers have been delighted to see the

footprints of a man on a barren shore, and we love to
see the waymarks of pilgrims while passing through the
vale of tears.[3]

This book is a collection of short accounts of some
of these eminent men and women who lost a beloved
child—who wept and who yet were comforted by the
Father of mercies. Spurgeon was right. The comfort they
obtained has helped me, and I believe that all who suffer
similar losses may discover these saints to be comrades
and find in their stories comfort and encouragement for
present distresses. But you must follow them all the way
to the path of glory. You may pause, but do not stop beside the graves of their loved ones. Follow them into the
Valley of Weeping, but do not stay there. Press ahead!
The path that leads to glory is the way of peace.

Many of the Christians remembered in the pages of
this work expressed their thoughts in verse. Poetry is the
language of the heart. In the poems collected here the emotions are raw and exposed. For example, Hetty Wesley
tells of a mother's grief and desire to follow her child in
death. Still, in general, you will find in these writers that
faith prevails over emotions. Emotions are based on what
we see, but faith on what we *know*. In the midst of trials,
particularly as we mourn the death of a loved one, we
must walk by faith and not by sight. Our eyes see defeat
in the corpse, the casket, and the grave. Yet by faith we
may say, 'Death is swallowed up in victory. O Death,

[3] C. H. Spurgeon, *Morning and Evening* (Uhrichsville, Ohio: Barbour
Publishing, 1998).

where is your sting? O Hades, where is your victory? . . .
Thanks be to God, who gives us the victory through our
Lord Jesus Christ" (*1 Cor.* 15:54-57).

A number of the poems are taken from old Christian
hymnals and express with beauty and eloquence the
intimate and personal reflections of each poet on the
death of a child. Echoing the words of Francis L. Patton
from more than a century ago, these hymn writers have

> taken the varied threads of human experience, woven
> them into a veil of exquisite texture and laid it across the
> face of death—in the seeming medley of earth's music,
> they have traced the love of Christ and found in it the
> motif that unified it all—leading us along the winding
> way of life, from light to dark, from dark to light again,
> until we enter the celestial city—leaving us there alone
> with God.[4]

With these things in mind, the tokens retold here are
offered (and may our Lord grant it) for the comfort of
others who know the loss of a child, whether young or
old, but particularly children of tender age. And I add
the prayer of the English Puritan Philip Doddridge that
'however weak and contemptible this work may seem in
the eyes of the children of this world, and however imper-

---

[4] Francis L. Patton, memorial discourse on A. A. Hodge, in A. A. Hodge,
Evangelical Theology (Edinburgh: Banner of Truth, 1976).

fect it really be, it may nevertheless live before Thee, and through a divine power be mighty to produce the rise and progress of religion.'

Should that be done, then let men say of this work that it has brought glory to God alone and that it is a worthy tribute to John Cameron Bruce. Here I borrow from Spurgeon and say of my son:

> Peace to his memory! I weave no fading wreath for his tomb, but I catch the gleaming of that immortal crown which the Master has placed upon his brow. He was a good boy, full of faith and of the Holy Spirit.

I also borrow from William Romaine's book, *The Life, Walk and Triumph of Faith,* and say:

> I present this book unto Thee, ever-glorious Jesus, and lay it at Thy feet. You know my heart; accept it graciously, as a public acknowledgment for inestimable mercies. In Thy great compassion overlook the faults in it; what is agreeable to the Scripture is Thine own. Make use of it to Thy praise. I devote myself, my body and soul, my tongue and pen, all I have and am, to Thy service. I would not look upon myself as any longer mine own, but being bought with a price, I would glorify Thee in the use of all Thy gifts and graces. With Thee I desire to walk through life. In Thine arms I hope to die.[5]

[5] William Romaine, *The Life, Walk and Triumph of Faith* (London: Charles J. Thynne, n.d.).

I want you to know, brethren, that the things which happened to me have actually turned out for the furtherance of the gospel.

THE APOSTLE PAUL (*Phil.* 1:12)

Part One

The Angel of Death

David said to his servants, 'Is the child dead?' And they said, 'He is dead.'

2 SAMUEL 12:19

*Small coffins are place in the ground,
but more than the body is buried.*

It is sad to watch parents bury their children. I have seen it and done it. Small coffins are placed in the ground, but more than the body is buried. Parents also bury all the hopes and dreams they had for those children. The mother buries the lullabies she would have sung, the little clothes, the first day at school; the father buries the baseball glove and thoughts of playing catch — all the things they see other parents doing and had hoped to do with their own sons and daughters. These losses are expressed well by Eugene Field's poem 'Little Boy Blue':

> *The little toy dog is covered with dust,*
> *But sturdy and staunch he stands;*
> *And the little toy soldier is red with rust,*
> *And his musket molds in his hands.*
> *Time was when the little toy dog was new,*
> *And the toy soldier was passing fair;*
> *And that was the time when our Little Boy Blue*
> *Kissed them and put them there.*
>
> *'Now, don't you go till I come', he said,*
> *'And don't you make any noise!'*
> *So, toddling off to his trundle-bed,*

> He dreamt of the pretty toys;
> And, as he was dreaming, an angel song
> Awakened our Little Boy Blue—
> Oh! the years are many, the years are long,
> But the little toy friends are true.
>
> Aye, faithful to Little Boy Blue they stand,
> Each in the same old place—
> Awaiting the touch of a little hand,
> The smile of a little face;
> And they wonder, as waiting the long years through
> In the dust of that little chair,
> What has become of our Little Boy Blue,
> Who kissed them and put them there.[1]

Dusty toy dogs and rusty toy soldiers pale before the glories of heaven, but they are present and profound losses just the same.

❧

> Wherefore should I make my moan,
>   Now the darling child is dead?
> He to early rest is gone,
>   He to paradise is fled.
> I shall go to him, but he
>   Never shall return to me.

[1] Eugene Field, *Lullaby-Land: Poems of Childhood* (New York: Charles Scribner's Sons, 1904).

God forbids his longer stay,
  God recalls the precious loan,
God hath taken him away,
  From my bosom to his own.
Surely what he wills is best!
  Happy in his will, I rest.

Faith cries out, it is the Lord!
  Let him do as seems him good.
Be thy holy name adored,
  Take the gift awhile bestowed;
Take the child no longer mine,
  Thine he is, forever thine.[2]

CHARLES WESLEY

---

[2] Charles Wesley, in *Hymn Book of the Methodist Episcopal Church, South* (Nashville: Publishing House of the Methodist Episcopal Church South, 1889).

. . . The stricken family stood round. In silent grief they were waiting the exit of the escaping spirit. All was hushed, solemn. No word was spoken. Each broken heart looked steadfastly on that loved form so soon to pass from their gaze forever. Ah! it was a moment of sad trial . . .

I

THE RIVER WITHOUT A BRIDGE

As I walked through the wilderness of this world, I lighted on a certain place where there was a den; and I laid down in that place to sleep: and as I slept, I dreamed a dream. I dreamed, and, behold, I saw a man dressed in rags, standing with his face from his own house, a book in his hand, and a great burden on his back. I looked, and saw him open the book; and as he read, he wept and trembled; then he broke out with a lamentable cry, saying, 'What shall I do?'

So begins the classic story of *The Pilgrim's Progress* as told by John Bunyan in 1678. It is the tale of a man named Christian and his long spiritual journey to the Celestial City of God. He starts out across a field, enters through the Narrow Gate, falls into the Slough of Despond, and passes under the Cross, where he loses the heavy burden on his back and experiences the forgiveness of his sins. Proceeding along the way, this pilgrim encounters many dangers—the Hill of Difficulty, wild beasts, and the dragon Apollyon. He is captured by Giant

Despair and imprisoned in Doubting Castle, from which he escapes with the Key of Promise.

Christian meets many worldly men, each one named according to the principal attribute of his character, such as Pliable, Obstinate, Formalist, and Hypocrisy. The pilgrim is also encouraged along the way by other valiant believers such as Faithful and Hopeful. Faithful is burned at the stake by the people of Vanity Fair and obtains a martyr's reward—a speedy entrance on a fiery chariot to the Celestial City.

At the end of the story, Christian and Hopeful come within view of the gates of heaven. 'I further saw in my dream', wrote Bunyan, 'that between them and the gate was a river, but there was no bridge to go over; and the river was very deep.' The two pilgrims enter the river, and Christian begins to sink in deep waters, the billowy waves going over his head. He exclaims, 'The sorrows of death have compassed about me!' Hopeful answers:

> These troubles and distresses that you go through in these waters are no sign that God has forsaken you; but they are sent to test you, to see whether you will recall that goodness, which up to now, you have received from Him and if you will live upon Him in your distresses. Be cheerful, Jesus Christ makes you whole.

With that, Bunyan saw in his dream Christian crying out in a loud voice, 'O! I see Him again, and He tells me, "When you pass through the waters, I will be with you; and through the rivers, they shall not overflow you."'

Then Christian and Hopeful both take courage; the enemy becomes as still as a stone, and so they cross over.

❧

Though the story is told in the 'similitude of a dream', it was more than that. The den in which the author slept was, in fact, Bunyan's jail cell. He spent twelve years in prison, as did many other Puritans during that era of England's history, and he suffered greatly for his faith. Had he recanted his religious convictions, perhaps he would have been released from jail. But he was willing to give up his life for the freedom to worship the Lord according to Scripture and his own conscience. For Bunyan, it was worth the cost.

Those were desperate times. Many Christians were banished from their homeland, others rotted in jail, and some were hanged. At one point Bunyan thought that he, too, would die in prison. In his autobiography, *Grace Abounding to the Chief of Sinners,* he wrote:

When I first began to think that my imprisonment might end at the gallows, I was greatly troubled. I was not fit to die, and I did not think I could if I were called to it. If I should climb the ladder to the noose with great difficulty, either quaking or showing other signs of fear, I would give the enemy a chance to disgrace the way of God and His people for their fearfulness. I was greatly troubled, for I was ashamed to die as a coward with tottering knees for such a cause as this.

So I was tossed about for many weeks, and knew not what to do. At last this thought came upon me with great weight: It was for the Word and the way of God that I was imprisoned, so I determined not to flinch at all. I also thought that God could choose whether He would give me comfort now or at the hour of death, but I could not choose whether or not to hold my profession. I was bound, but He was free; yes, it was my duty to stand to His Word, whether or not He would ever look upon me or save me at the last. With this thought, I was for going on, and venturing my eternal state with Christ, whether I have comfort here or not. If God does not come in, I will still leap off the ladder even blindfolded into eternity, sink or swim, come heaven, come hell. Lord Jesus, catch me if You will; if not, I will still risk my life for Thy name.[1]

With the stakes so high, we can hardly imagine the emotional stress upon Bunyan. Not only did he have concerns for his own life, but he was deeply affected by the burdens that would be placed upon his family—a wife, Elizabeth, and four children. He described his anguish in the following passage:

I found myself a man full of weakness. Parting with my wife and poor children has often been to me in this place as the pulling of flesh from my bones, because I often thought about the many hardships, miseries and needs

---

[1] John Bunyan, *Grace Abounding to the Chief of Sinners*, in *Works of John Bunyan* (Edinburgh: Banner of Truth, 1991).

that my poor family would likely meet with, should I be taken from them, especially my poor blind child, who lay nearer my heart than all I had besides; O the hardship I thought my blind one might go under would break my heart to pieces. Poor child, what sorrow are you likely to have for your portion in this world? You will be beaten and suffer hunger, cold, nakedness, and a thousand calamities, though I cannot now endure even the wind to blow upon you. But I must place you all in God's care, though it breaks my heart to leave you. O, I was as a man who was pulling down his house upon the head of his wife and children; yet I must do it, I must do it.[2]

Bunyan's wife bravely appeared in court to plead for his release from jail. 'I have', she told the judges, 'four small children that cannot help themselves; one is blind, and we have nothing to live upon, but the charity of good people. I was pregnant when my husband was first arrested. I was dismayed at the news, fell into labour and was delivered, but my child died.' Her pleas for her husband's release fell on deaf ears.

Though Bunyan was a prolific author, he did not leave us any specific words about the death of this child who was born prematurely. He did, however, write about his belief that God is well able to save children:

[2] Ibid.

Although they are children, God can deal with them as with John the Baptist, and cause them in a moment to leap for joy of Christ; or else save them by His grace, as He saves His other elect infants. He may thus comprehend them, though they cannot apprehend Him. God comforted Rachel concerning her children that Herod murdered because of the birth of Christ. He bids her not to cry with the promise that her children would come again from the land of the enemy, from death. And I think this should be mentioned, not only for her and their sakes, but to comfort all those that either have had, or yet may have, their children suffer for righteousness. None of these things happen without the determinate counsel of God. He has ordained the sufferings of little children as well as that of persons more in years. And it is easy to think that God can as well foresee which of his elect shall suffer by violent hands in their infancy, as which of them shall then die a natural death. He has saints small in age as well as in esteem. And although I desire not to see these days again, yet it will please me to see those little ones that suffer for Jesus, standing in their white robes with the elders of their people, before the throne, singing unto the Lamb.[3]

Bunyan's story does not end here. Death would again strike him a blow and take another child—his poor, blind Mary. Here is the death scene as found in the old book

[3] John Bunyan, *Advice to Sufferers*, in *Works of John Bunyan* (Edinburgh: Banner of Truth, 1991).

Mary Bunyan, The Dreamer's Blind Daughter: A Tale of Religious Persecution:

The sun was low in the west. The sweet, fresh air of heaven stole in through the open windows. On a low cot, where the rays of the setting sun fell over the thin, wasted form, lay Mary Bunyan with closed eyes, her bosom scarcely moved by the slow, faint breath. The stricken family stood round. In silent grief they were waiting the exit of the escaping spirit. All was hushed and solemn. No word was spoken. Each broken heart looked steadfastly on that loved form so soon to pass from their gaze forever. Ah! it was a moment of sad trial, but it was also a time of humble submission.

The thin hand moves upward. The sightless eyes open and turn to heaven. The pale lips murmur, 'Come, Lord Jesus, come quickly.' Then there steals over the colourless face a smile of ineffable beauty. The hands fall motionless on the bosom;—a gasp—a breath—all is ended.

The wasted form is there. The spirit, borne by angels, is ushered into the presence of the Great King. Now the poor blind girl sees even as she is seen, knows even as she is known. A crown and a harp are given her, and she joins with rapturous ecstasy in the song of Moses and the Lamb.

Subdued weeping is heard throughout the room. The holy man of God kneels beside the inanimate form, and prays the blessing of God on himself and these stricken ones. The next day the neighbors and friends gathered in, and the remains of the poor blind girl were borne from the little cottage, and deposited beside those of her mother in the burying ground of the church. From this sad event Bunyan never entirely recovered. It was a dark shadow all along his pathway until he, too, came to lie down peacefully in the silent tomb.[4]

In his book *Advice to Sufferers*, Bunyan wrote about suffering loss and where comfort is to be sought—where he found peace that consoled all the griefs of this life:

> God consoles His suffering people, and His consolations, which are proportioned to the nature and degree of their suffering, shall surely appear to all who stick to His truth and trust Him with their souls. It is a demonstration of the faithfulness of God to those that, suffering according to His will, do commit the keeping of their souls to Him in well-doing, as unto a faithful Creator (*1 Peter* 4:19).

[4] Sallie R. Ford, *Mary Bunyan, The Dreamer's Blind Daughter: A Tale of Religious Persecution* (New York: Sheldon & Company, 1860; repr. Swengel: Reiner Publications, 1976).

And behold, there came a man . . . and he fell down at Jesus'
feet, and begged Him to come to his house; for he had an
only daughter about twelve years of age, and she was dying.
LUKE 8:41-42

I am happy in spirit, but the flesh is sorrowful and will
not be content; the parting grieves me beyond measure.
MARTIN LUTHER

The school of faith is said to go about with death.
MARTIN LUTHER

2

A FATHER'S LAST EMBRACE

Martin Luther was the German reformer who reclaimed, after centuries of religious darkness, the light of Scripture and the Christian doctrine of justification by faith alone—'the truth by which the church either stands or falls.' Against kings and councils, to the peril of his own life, he raised the banners of the Protestant Reformation: Sola Scriptura (Scripture Alone), Solus Christus (Christ Alone), Sola Gratia (Grace Alone), Sola Fide (Faith Alone), and Sola Deo Gloria (To God Alone Be the Glory). 'Here I stand', said Luther. 'I can do no other; God help me.'

Luther's resolve and constant devotion to biblical truth may also be seen in the story of the death of his daughter Magdalene in September of 1542:

As his daughter lay very ill, Dr Luther said: 'I love her very much, but dear God, if it be Thy will to take her, I submit to Thee.' Then he said to her as she lay in bed: 'Magdalene, my dear little daughter, would you like to stay here with your father, or would you willingly go to your Father yonder?' She answered: 'Darling father, as God wills.' Then he said, 'Dearest child, the spirit is willing but the flesh is weak.' Then he turned away and said: 'I love her very much; if my flesh is so strong, what can my spirit do? God has given no bishop so great a gift in a thousand years as he has given me in her. I am angry with myself that I cannot rejoice in heart and be thankful as I ought.'

Now as Magadalene lay in agony of death, her father fell down before the bed on his knees and wept bitterly and prayed that God might free her. Then she departed and fell asleep in her father's arms. As they laid her in the coffin he said: 'Darling Lena, you will rise and shine like a star, yea, like the sun. I am happy in spirit, but the flesh is sorrowful and will not be content, the parting grieves me beyond measure. I have sent a saint to heaven.'[1]

The death of his daughter did not dampen Luther's love and fervent devotion to God. Later during his last illness, though he felt great pain, he talked with his friends to the last about the happiness of the future world and of meeting again hereafter. When his pain began to increase and death approached, he called for Justus Jonas, a fellow reformer, who heard him repeat three times, 'Father, into

---

[1] Preserved Smith, ed., *The Life and Letters of Martin Luther* (London: J. Murray, 1911).

Thy hand I commend my spirit. Thou hast redeemed me, O God of Truth!' and say the following prayer:

> My dear heavenly Father, eternal, merciful God! Thou hast revealed unto me thy beloved Son, our Lord Jesus Christ; him have I taught and confessed, him I love and honor as my dear Savior and Redeemer, whom the wicked persecute, despise and revile. Take my soul to thyself![2]

When the marks of approaching death appeared in his face, Jonas asked Luther, 'Reverend Father, will you stand firm in Christ, and upon the doctrine which you have preached?' Luther answered, 'Yes!' and fell into a soft sleep and died. His daughter did not return to him, but he went to her.

[2] Clyde L. Manschreck, *Melanchthon: The Quiet Reformer* (New York: Abingdon Press, 1958).

Ah! when the mighty wings of the angel of death nestle over your heart's treasures, and his black shadow broods over your home, it shakes the heart with a shuddering terror and a horror of great darkness . . . As I stand by the little grave, and think of the poor ruined clay within, that was a few days ago so beautiful, my heart bleeds. But as I ask, 'Where is the soul whose beams gave that clay all its beauty and preciousness?' I triumph.

ROBERT L. DABNEY

3

THE CRUEL DESTROYER

Dr Robert L. Dabney is remembered today by some for his service with General Thomas 'Stonewall' Jackson during the American Civil War, his work as a theologian, and his role in the founding of a Presbyterian seminary. In the fall of 1855, he set out on a 140-mile trip to attend a church synod meeting in North Carolina. The trees were perhaps still in their brilliant autumn colors, but Dabney paid little attention; his thoughts were mostly on his little boy, Robert (whom he affectionately called Bobby). His son was sick, and Dabney had hesitated about starting his trip.

From the time his father left, Bobby grew rapidly worse. Dabney received word that his son was extremely ill with 'a putrid sore throat that threatened suffocation'. Dabney turned back and travelled all night, reaching home the next evening. What followed next is best retold in Dabney's own words in a letter to his brother:

> We used prompt measures, and sent early for the doctor, who did not think his case was dangerous; but he grew gradually worse until Sunday, when his symptoms

became alarming, and he passed away, after great sufferings, Monday. He was intelligent to the end, even after
he became speechless, and his appealing looks to us and
the physician would have melted a stone. A half hour
before he died, he sank into a sleep, which became more
and more quiet, until he gently sighed his soul away. This
is the first death we have had in our family, and my first
experience of any great sorrow. I have learned rapidly
in the school of anguish this week, and am many years
older than I was a few days ago. It was not so much
that I could not give my darling up, but that I saw him
suffer such pangs, and then fall under the grasp of the
cruel destroyer, while I was impotent for his help. Ah!
when the mighty wings of the angel of death nestle over
your heart's treasures, and his black shadow broods
over your home, it shakes the heart with a shuddering
terror and a horror of great darkness. To see my dear
little one ravaged, crushed and destroyed, turning his
beautiful liquid eyes to me and his weeping mother for
help, after his gentle voice could no longer be heard, and
to feel myself as helpless to give any aid—this tears my
heart with anguish.[1]

Dabney's son died of diphtheria, not two weeks from
the death of another son, Jimmy, who had died from the

[1] Thomas Cary Johnson, *The Life and Letters of Robert Lewis Dabney*
(Edinburgh: Banner of Truth, 1977).

same disease. It has been said of Dabney that in these bereavements he suffered as only a very strong man, a man of persistence and intensity of character, could suffer. But the deaths of the two boys wore hard upon him. One of his seminary students wrote at this time:

> Among the most gloomy days that occurred during my seminary course were the ones when his children, James and Robert, died and were buried. They were 'rare and radiant' little boys, and they had a warm place in my heart. There was only a brief interval between their funerals. In the many burial scenes I have witnessed, Dabney was about the only heart-broken mourner, without visible tears, that I have ever seen. Before that, I had never realized the deep and almost unearthly significance of a sorrow too deep for tears. At the burial of Robert, there was something in Dabney's features so pallid and deathly, as he took a parting look at his dead first-born child . . . In a little while, however, we were glad to see him emerge from the gloom of this afflictive time and resume his duties with quickened zeal and impressive unction.[2]

Dabney fought to save his sons' lives, and that should not go unnoticed. Death is a not a friend to be embraced, but an ugly enemy, a vile intruder into the world. But God,

[2] Ibid.

in his common grace, gives us doctors and medicines, and we should use them to treat illnesses, adding our prayers for God's blessings upon such treatment for the restoration of the body's health. And more than that, we should give thanks to God, who has conquered death through the resurrection of his Son, Jesus Christ. Because of him, death has no sting or victory over the children of God.

Dabney picked up this thought later in the same letter to his brother, saying:

> Our parting is not for long. This spoiled and ruined body will be raised, and all its ravished beauties more than repaired. As for my other loved ones, whom I see exposed to disease and death, I know that death cannot touch them unless my Heavenly Father, who orders everything for me in love and wisdom, sees it best. So that I can trust them, though trembling, to His keeping, and be at peace. Our little Jimmy, we hope and trust, is now a ransomed spirit . . . This is a hope inexpressible and full of glory. As I stand by the little grave, and think of the poor ruined clay within, that was a few days ago so beautiful, my heart bleeds. But as I ask, 'Where is the soul whose beams gave that clay all its beauty and preciousness?' I triumph. Has it not already begun, with an infant voice, the praises of my Savior? Perhaps one of the loving angels that bore home his spirit has been teaching and training him to heavenly manhood. Perhaps he has been committed to our sainted father, or to my wife's sainted grandmother, as one of their redeemed posterity, to keep and train till we can embrace him

again. At any rate, he is in Christ's heavenly house and under His guardian love. Now I feel, as never before, the blessedness of the redeeming grace and divine blood, which have ransomed my poor babe from all the sin and death which he inherited through me.[3]

This is not the end of Dabney's tale; more of him will be told later. But I must say here that of all men remembered in this book, I see more of myself in Dabney's story—though I'm not half the man Dabney was. He, more than all the others, expressed so much of what I have experienced: a sick little boy, casting his eyes upon me and my wife, an occasional cry but with no sound because of the ventilator tube in his mouth, and I was impotent to help. I buried John Cameron's body in a little grave, and my heart bleeds, though I triumph in the hope that his soul is present with our Saviour. Dabney's example will lead us further along the path to glory. I follow, though in unequal steps.

[3] Ibid.

Many know how fondly I loved my daughter; and this love has not been extinguished by her death, but continues to be nourished by sorrow and ardent desires.

PHILIP MELANCHTHON

4

MORE EPITAPHS

PHILIP MELANCHTHON

Philip Melanchthon was another pillar of the German-led Reformation. He was a close friend of Martin Luther. Melanchthon's second son, George, died at the age of two. Some weeks following the boy's death, Luther described Melanchthon's state of mind in a letter to Justus Jonas: 'Philip is still grieving. We all sympathize with him, as a man of worth richly deserves it.'

Nearly twenty years later, Melanchthon's firstborn, a daughter named Anna, died. She left behind a husband and four children. Philip expressed his anguish in a letter to a friend: 'I send you a narrative of my daughter's death, which, whenever I read it, or even just think of it, so increases my parental sorrow, that I fear it will injure my health. I cannot banish the sight of my weeping daughter from my eyes.' Melanchthon also sent a letter to comfort his son-in-law:

I wish our friendship to be a lasting one, and I am determined to cherish it faithfully. I shall look upon your children as my own, and they are indeed my own. I do not love them less than I loved their mother. Many know how fondly I loved my daughter; and this love has not been extinguished by her death, but continues to be nourished by sorrow and ardent desires. And as I know how much she loved her children, I believe that I must show them those same affections myself.[1]

The following correspondence was later sent by Melanchthon to encourage a friend whose son had died, and so the comforted became a comforter:

God has implanted the principle of natural affection in mankind, for the double purpose of strengthening the bonds of human society, and teaching us to realize the warmth and fervour of His love to His own Son and to us. He therefore approves the affection we cherish for our offspring, and the piety of our grief for their loss. But you are well aware that we are not permitted to mourn unduly. It is certain that these events are under divine oversight and direction; we would do well, therefore, to submit to God, and quietly resign ourselves to His control in every season of adversity.

Wise men have often inquired with astonishment as to why the feeble nature of man is oppressed with such weight of afflictions; but we who can trace the causes to a divine origin, should yield without resistance to

[1] *Melanchthon: The Quiet Reformer.*

the decrees of God, and avail ourselves of the remedies for grief which He, in divine goodness, has revealed. Remember that 'in Him we live and move and have our being.'[2]

❦

C. H. SPURGEON

One of the brightest, bonniest babies ever seen, he was the delight and expectation of our hearts; but the gift was claimed suddenly, and the child, who was to have done, according to our ideas, so much service on earth, went to sing God's praises with the angels!

MRS C. H. SPURGEON

Charles Spurgeon was perhaps the preeminent Baptist preacher of nineteenth-century England. In his later ministry, he fought to keep the Baptist church from departing from the doctrines of historic Christianity. He counselled his young students to be faithful to the Lord Jesus Christ and the doctrines of his grace.

In the spring of 1886, Spurgeon wrote to a friend (a trusted deacon who served with him at the Metropolitan Tabernacle). To this friend who had lost a child through death, Spurgeon said:

[2] Ibid.

I feel very grieved for you and your dear wife, for I know your tender hearts. Yet the bitterest elements of sorrow are not in the cup, for we have no doubt as to where the little ones must be. You now have a child among the angels—to whom we will soon go. So short is life that our wounds are healed almost as soon as they begin to bleed. We part, and so soon meet again. Mrs Spurgeon joins with me in loving sympathy.[3]

Spurgeon and his wife Susannah had twin sons, Charles and Thomas. A few years after writing to his deacon-friend, Spurgeon once again took up his pen to comfort grieving parents—this time his own son and daughter-in-law:

My dear Children,

The Lord himself comfort you. I want comforting myself. To think of that dear little creature being taken away! It must be right! It must be good! Our Father is never mistaken nor unkind . . . I feel sure you will both find a secret strength poured into your souls, and in this also faith shall have the victory.

[3] Iain H. Murray ed., *Letters of C. H. Spurgeon* (Edinburgh: Banner of Truth, 1992).

I shall never forget the day. . . . To you it must be a sharp cut; but our Lord has an almighty salve.[4]

> Your loving father,
> C. H. Spurgeon

Less than two years after that sad day, Charles Spurgeon died. Remembering both the deceased lad and his grandfather, Mrs Spurgeon wrote:

Ah, me! it was not so long ago that the oldest of my twin-boys brought his firstborn son, and my beloved husband, in one of those tender outpourings of the heart which were so natural to him, gave the child to God. Not many months afterwards—God answered the prayer, and took the child to himself! One of the brightest, bonniest babies ever seen, he was the delight and expectation of our hearts; but the gift was claimed suddenly, and the child, who we thought would do so much service on earth, went to sing God's praises with the angels! I wonder, sometimes, whether the little ransomed spirit met and welcomed his warrior grandfather on the shores of the Glory-land![5]

With such a firm hope of the child's entrance into heaven, Mrs Spurgeon mirrored the thoughts of her preacher-husband who said,

We are convinced that all who die in infancy share in the redemption worked out by our Lord Jesus. Whatever

[4] Ibid.
[5] *C. H. Spurgeon, Autobiography, Vol. I: The Early Years* (Edinburgh: Banner of Truth, 1985).

others may think, we believe that the whole spirit and tone of the Word of God, as well as the nature of God himself, lead us to believe that all who leave this world as babes are saved.

JOHANN SEBASTIAN BACH

What'er my God ordains is right;
here shall my stand be taken;
Though sorrow, need, or death be mine,
Yet I am not forsaken.
My Father's care is round me there;
He holds me that I shall not fall;
And so to Him I leave it all.

SAMUEL RODIGAST

Johann Sebastian Bach was a master musician who left us a wealth of worship music of the highest order and beauty. After composing a piece of music, he often closed his manuscript with the initials 'S.D.G.' (*Soli Deo Gloria*—'To God Alone Be Glory'). Many of his works also began with the abbreviation 'J.J.' (*Jesu Juva* or 'Jesus, help me').

It is not so well known today that Bach was a bereaved parent. In fact, he was married twice (his first wife predeceased him), and of the twenty children born of his two marriages, he saw thirteen of them carried to the grave.

Bach did his best to instill courage into his second wife's suffering heart by giving her a music book. Three times he wrote into the book variations of a simple tune he composed for her based on the hymn 'Fret Not, My Soul; on God Rely.'

Despite the grief that surely must have characterized much of his life, Bach was able to raise his thoughts to the grandeur and majesty of Christ, and from his pen flowed hymns of praise like the familiar 'Jesu, Joy of Man's Desiring' and 'My Heart Ever Faithful', the latter of which has the following verse:

> *My heart ever faithful, sing praises, be joyful;*
> *Sing praises, be joyful, thy Jesus is near.*
> *Away with complaining, away with complaining,*
> *Faith ever maintaining, my Jesus is near.*

A favorite text of Bach for his church music was Samuel Rodigast's hymn 'What'er My God Ordains Is Right'. The words of this hymn offer great comfort and counsel for grieving parents:

> *What-e'er my God ordains is right;*
> *His holy will abideth;*
> *I will be still what-e'er He doth,*
> *and follow where He guideth.*
> *He is my God; though dark my road,*
> *He holds me that I shall not fall;*
> *Wherefore to Him I leave it all.*

What'er my God ordains is right;
He never will deceive me;
He leads me by the proper path;
I know He will not leave me,
I take, content, what He hath sent;
His hand can turn my griefs away,
And patiently I wait His day.

What'er my God ordains is right;
though now this cup, in drinking,
May bitter seem to my faint heart,
I take it, all unshrinking.
My God is true; each morn anew,
sweet comfort yet shall fill my heart,
And pain and sorrow shall depart.

What'er my God ordains is right;
here shall my stand be taken;
Though sorrow, need, or death be mine,
yet am I not forsaken.
My Father's care is round me there;
He holds me that I shall not fall,
And so to Him I leave it all.[6]

Oh, to have such simple, childlike trust in God as Father. Every day we who have lost children should remember the example of Bach and pray, 'Jesus, help me', as we rise from bed and, 'Glory to God alone', when the day is done.

[6] Samuel Rodigast, in *Trinity Hymnal* (Philadelphia: Great Commission Publications, 1982).

✺

John Bradford

To the tune of 'Death of the Son'
A Psalm of David

I will praise You, O Lord, with my whole heart;
I will tell of all Your marvellous works.
I will be glad and rejoice in You;
I will sing praise to Your name,
> *O Most High.*

Psalm 9:1-2

. . . carry Christ's cross, as he shall lay it upon your back.

John Bradford

During an awful time of persecution in the middle of the sixteenth century, God raised up a remnant of men and women in England who were valiant for truth and for the cause of Christ. One of these godly men, John Bradford, wrote a letter to a woman to encourage her, knowing that her son would soon be chained to a stake and die a fiery death. The woman was his own mother, and he the son. The following are selections from his letter:

My most dear mother,

In the compassion of Christ I heartily pray and beseech you to be thankful for me unto God, who now takes me unto Himself. I die not, my good mother, as a thief, a murderer, or adulterer; but I die as a witness of Christ, His gospel, and truth, which I have confessed. I thank God, though I am imprisoned, I am even willing to confirm it by fire. Therefore, my good and most dear mother, give thanks for me to God, that He has made your son to be a witness of His glory. Pray often and continually to God the Father, through Christ; hearken to the Scriptures; serve God after His Word, and not after custom; carry Christ's cross, as He shall lay it upon your back; forgive them that kill me; pray for them, for they know not what they do; commit my cause to God our Father; be mindful of both your daughters, to help them as you can.

I have nothing to give you or to leave behind for you, except that I pray to God my Father, for His Christ's sake, that He would bless you and keep you from evil. May He give you patience; may He make you thankful, for me and for yourself, that He will take your child to witness His truthfulness. I confess to the whole world that I die and leave this life, in hope of one much better, which I look for at the hands of God my Father through the merits of His dear Son, Jesus Christ.

So, my dear mother, I say my last farewell to you in this life, beseeching the almighty and eternal Father, by Christ, to grant that we may meet in the life to come, where we shall give Him continual thanks and praise for ever and ever. Amen.

Your son in the Lord,
John Bradford[7]

This letter reminds us of One even greater than John Bradford—Jesus Christ, who comforted his own mother in the hour of his death upon the cross. Remember John 19:26-27: 'When Jesus therefore saw his mother, and the disciple whom he loved standing by, he said to his mother, "Woman, behold your son!" Then he said to the disciple, "Behold your mother!" And from that hour that disciple took her to his own home.'

Of this great moment in our Lord's Passion, Matthew Henry comments:

> See here an instance of divine goodness, to be observed for our encouragement. Sometimes when God removes one comfort from us, he raises up another for us, perhaps where we did not look for it.[8]

This was abundantly true for our family after the death of John Cameron. Because an inherited genetic disorder caused our son's illness, we decided not to have any more children of our own, but we were open to the idea of

---

[7] Letter 48 in the Christian Classics Ethereal Library, www.ccel.org/b/bradford/writings/letters.html#_Toc429906107.
[8] Matthew Henry, *Commentary on the Whole Bible* (Grand Rapids: Zondervan, repr. 1988).

adoption. We applied to an adoption agency, but God had other plans for us and raised up another son through my wife's work with a support network for parents who have children in Neonatal Intensive Care Units—not the typical avenue for would-be adoptive parents.

While we were focusing our eyes on the adoption agency, God was putting my wife, Joni, in a place to meet a woman who knew of a young mother who planned to place her unborn child up for adoption. Joni shared with this woman about our deceased son and our hope to adopt another child. Through the help of this lady, within a matter of weeks, we brought home a newborn boy who is now our adopted son. So God raised up another son for us. This boy has been a comfort for us as grieving parents, and for our daughter, who so much wanted to be a big sister. All this came from a place where we did not look. 'God works in a mysterious way, His wonders to perform!'

Part Two

The Valley of Weeping

My groanings pour out like water. For the thing I greatly feared has come upon me, and what I dreaded has happened to me. I am not at ease, nor am I quiet; I have no rest, for trouble comes.

Job 3:24-26

Ah, regard a mother's moan!
Anguish deeper than thy own.
HETTY WESLEY

5

A Mother's Moan

What lies beyond the cemetery is the valley of weeping. Even before we leave our child's grave, we have begun the journey into that valley. Only, we do not know how deep or how wide the valley is, and this can make the descent both sad and fearful. Worse yet, if we are married, our spouse will also be in the valley. And though we enter together, we may not stay together. Often, one spouse will take a different path and, perhaps, go to places lower than the other can follow. Thankfully, there is a faithful Guide, a Good Shepherd to lead us through the valley.

❦

Hetty Wesley was a sister of the well-known Charles and John Wesley. All three of her children died in infancy. She wrote this poem after the death of her last child:

> *Tender softness, infant mild,*
> *Perfect, purest, brightest child!*
> *Transient lustre, beauteous clay,*
> *Smiling wonder of a day!*

Ere the last convulsive start
Rend thy unresisting heart,
Ere the long-enduring swoon
Weigh thy precious eyelids down,
Ah, regard a mother's moan!
Anguish deeper than thy own.

Ere thy gentle breast sustain
Latest, fiercest, mortal pain,
Here a suppliant! Let me be
Partner in thy destiny:
That whene'er the fatal cloud
Must thy radiant temples shroud;
When deadly damps, impending now,
Shall hover round thy destined brow,
Diffusive may their influence be,
And with the blossom blast the tree![1]

Hetty Wesley expressed the deep, heart-wrenching sorrow that some parents, particularly mothers, feel when their children's bodies are laid in the grave. Real grief is not easily comforted. It comes like ocean waves rushing up the sand, subsiding back, only to roll in again. These waves vary in size, frequency, and intensity. Some are small, lapping up around the feet. Others are stronger; they foam the water around you and cause you to stagger. Then there are the overwhelming waves with an undertow that can turn your world upside down and drag you

[1] Quoted in Sir Arthur Quiller-Couch, *Hetty Wesley* (London: Harper, 1903).

out into deep waters. In times such as those, the mourner desperately needs an anchor. And, indeed, God has promised his people a blessing if they patiently endure. He has guaranteed the promise so that we might lay hold of the hope set before us. This hope is the anchor of the soul, and it is sure and steadfast (*Heb.* 6:19).

❧

One of these waves hit my wife about seven months after John Cameron's death. It was the season of Thanksgiving, but not for her. The grief of losing a son was mixed with the desire for another child. Desire turned to near despair when we decided not to have any more children. But what neither she nor I could see at the time was the place that God was preparing for us. The new 'place' was the life that awaited us with our adopted son. And while God was preparing a place for us, he was also preparing us for the place. Our house of mourning would become a house of rejoicing, but we were not yet through the Valley of Weeping.

No doubt affliction now seems to you a far more intense and real thing than it ever did before; the griefs of human life are far more awful and terrific to you now than they ever before seemed. But the power of grace is the master of them. . . .

LETTER FROM A FRIEND TO
DR ROBERT DABNEY

6

A Dagger Of Ice

Deep, intense grief is no respecter of persons. Man or woman, rich or poor, young or old—there is no difference. Abraham Lincoln said of his own son Willie: 'I know that he is much better off in Heaven, but then we loved him so. It is hard, hard to have him die!' Recall Dr Robert Dabney's loss of two sons within the space of just one month. Not long after this tragedy Dabney wrote a letter to his brother about his grief and, strangely, about his fears in showing affection to a surviving child:

> It is painful to me to write to my friends now, delightful as it is to receive their letters. I cannot speak of anything except that which fills my mind every waking hour (except when I drag it away to my daily work)—my two boys gone from me; and yet it is painful to speak of them, too.
>
> When my Jimmy died, the grief was painfully sharp, but the actings of faith, the embracing of consolation, and all the cheering truths which ministered comfort to me were just as vivid; but when the stroke was repeated, and thereby doubled, I seem to be paralyzed and stunned. I know that my loss is doubled, and I know also that

the same cheering truths apply to the second as to the first, but I remain numb, downcast, almost without hope and interest. When I turned away from Jimmy's corpse to my lovely infant, my affections and fears seemed to flow out towards him with a strength both sweet and agonizing. I never tired of folding him in my arms, as the sweet substitute for my loss, nor of trembling for him also, lest the loss should extend to him. But when Bobby was taken, and our little one remained our only hope, it seemed to me, I was both afraid and reluctant to center my affections on him. I feel towards him a mixture of weak, listless feelings and pain, not having the heart to be happy in his caresses, and not daring. This is strange, perhaps inexplicable. Death has struck me with a dagger of ice.[1]

Dabney had a strong faith and a good hope that his two sons were with the Lord. 'Yet believing this as I do firmly', he wrote, 'I hardly have life to rejoice in it.' His constant prayer was that he could see in the blows caused by these events some blessing to himself, his family, and friends; for then in time he thought that he would be able to bless God for them. He hoped, too, that he would be more faithful in striving to do good to his friends.

When news of Jimmy's death reached a friend of Dabney's, the friend wrote to him:

Your loss is great; but the grace of your Master is very, very great. Your noble boy is gone. I remember him. But he sleeps. Let the Master have him.

[1] *The Life and Letters of Robert Lewis Dabney.*

After the death of Bobby, the same friend wrote again. His letter is worthy of the following lengthy quote:

My heart is sad for you, my brother. Your two bright and noble boys, both gone! What a grief! What an overwhelming sorrow! God is in this matter, moving amid the cloud and darkness of a throne which is nevertheless all spotless and full of glory. It is a case in which you must trust God, and trust him utterly. This is easy to say, but in the intensity and great force of the conditions which agitate your heart, it is no doubt difficult for you to see into the full significance, the deep and powerful force of the idea. Yet there is, for all that, a ground for your trusting in him, though he slay you.

No doubt affliction now seems to you a far more intense and real thing than it ever did before; the griefs of human life are far more awful and terrific to you now than they ever before seemed. But the power of grace is the master of them, and as you feel with such intensity the power of the ill, do not allow it to fill up your soul so as to exclude the other truth.

Steady your spirit in the storm for an instant, and fix your attention on the fact that, awful as is the grief which darkens your house, yet there is a power to master it, and that no matter how fearful may be the trouble, it may be cast upon the Lord; no matter how great the tribulation, you may still rejoice in it.

Has your Christian hope been blown out by the tempest? Have you questioned whether God could deal with you like this if you were his child? If you have, it is a natural, but not a sound conclusion. Was not Job beloved of God at the very time when his children perished? Do not give up your trust in him; wait, bow, submit—submit even to bear the rage of your own unbelief, and say to him, 'Even amid my agony, yet I will trust in thee, though thou slay me, too.'

I do hope and pray that God may give you grace to exercise a faith which will humble, comfort and cheer your inmost soul. But if you cannot so believe, at least lay your hands on your bleeding and darkened spirit, and drag it along the way of duty. Follow the Master's will, in comfort if you can, but follow it. He will bring you out into a pleasant place in his own time.[2]

❧

Four years later Dabney saw an answer to his earlier prayers. He travelled to Georgetown to address a Bible Society. While there he learned of a couple whose little boy—an only child—was sick with fever. Without hesitation, he accepted an invitation to meet with the family. An eyewitness reported that Dabney gently walked through the house to the back parlour where the child was lying. The mother was on her knees near the child. Dabney stood still and silently took in the whole scene. Soon he walked to the bed, knelt beside the mother, and gave way to a flood of tears. Then he offered a prayer for the parents and the boy—a prayer that could only have come

[2] Ibid.

from one capable of empathizing with the family's affliction. He arose, repeated some suitable and tender words
of the Saviour, and departed.

Within a few days, the child was buried. Afterwards
the mother reported that Dr Dabney's visit did her more
good than all the visits and prayers of all other friends.
Here is empathy in action—one person appreciating the
pain of another, then coming alongside to help. The cruel
destroyer had brought death to the Dabney family. But
God brought blessings to the grieving father, and through
him, to others.

A few years later Robert Dabney once again entered
into the Valley of Weeping. In the early years of the
American Civil War, Dabney took a post as chief of
Stonewall Jackson's staff. The hard army life took its toll
on Major Dabney. He fell ill with a fever and returned
home. While he was lying sick, diphtheria again attacked
his children. His sons—Charles, Thomas, and Samuel—
all had it. Eight days after taking ill, and with very great
suffering, Thomas died. Dabney spoke of the little boy as
one of the brightest of his sons.

He retells the story of his little Tom's death in a mag-
nificent poem entitled 'Tried, but Comforted'. In the
words of Francis Patton, Dabney wove the threads of his
own experience into a beautiful veil that he laid across the
face of death.

Five summers bright our noble boy
Was lent us for our household joy;
Then came the fated, wintry hour
Of death, and blighted our sweet flower.

They told me, 'Weep not, for thy gem
Is fixed in Christ's own diadem;
His speedy feet the race have run,
The foe have 'scaped, the goal have won.'

I chode the murmurs of my breast
With this dear thought; and then addressed
My steps to wait upon the Lord
And with his saints to hear His Word.

Then, thus I heard their anthem flow:
'Praise Him, all creatures here below;
Praise Him above, ye heavenly host;
Praise Father, Son, and Holy Ghost.'

But how, I said, can this sad heart,
In joyful praises bear its part?
It hath no joy; it naught can do
But mourn its loss and tell its woe.

And then I thought, What if thy lost
Is now among that heavenly host,
And with the angel choir doth sing,
'Glory to Thee, Eternal King?'

But is not this a hope too sweet?
Faith is too weak the joy to meet;
Oh! might my bursting heart but see
If true the blissful thought can be!

Oh! that for once mine ear might hear
That tiny voice, so high, so clear,
Singing Emmanuel's name among
Those louder strains, that mightier throng.

Oh! that but once mine eyes could see
That smile which here was wont to be
The sunshine of my heart, made bright
With Jesus' love, with Heaven's light.

Then would my burdened heart, I know,
With none but tears of joy o'erflow—
But ah! when faith would strain her eyes
For that blest vision, there arise

The shadows of my dreary home;
'Twixt Heaven and my heart there come
That dying bed, that corpse, that bier;
And when I strive that song to hear,

Sad memory echoes but the wail
My love to soothe could naught avail;
I only hear his anguished cry,
I only see his glazing eye.

But yet be still, tumultuous heart,
And bravely bear thy destined part,
Yet will I say, stay there, my son;
And to my Lord, Thy will be done.

'Tis not for sight and sense to know
Those scenes of glory here below;
But be it ours to walk by faith,
And credit what our Savior saith.

Let patience work till we be meet
To dwell in bliss at Jesus' feet;
Then death, once dreaded, friendly come,
And bear us to our lost one's home.

Then shall that glorious hour repay
The woes of all that dreary way,
And I shall hear forever more
My seraph boy his God adore.

Yea, he shall teach this voice to raise,
As angels taught him, Heaven's lays;
And I, who once his steps did lead,
Shall follow him to Christ, our Head.

Dabney died on January 3, 1898; he was an old man, infirm and blind. He had instructed his remaining sons to bury him in a little cemetery that belonged to Union Theological Seminary, where he had taught for so many years as Professor of Theology. It has been written that 'he loved a particular spot in that cemetery because his great heart had broken once, twice, thrice at a child's grave, and he would have his body sleep beside the bodies of his three little sons till the resurrection morning.'

Dabney's life and ministry are all but forgotten today. But of all the men whose lives are recounted in this book, his testimony has most touched my own heart. What amazes me is how he never lost sight of the ultimate goal of life or of the union he had with the One in whom we live and move and have our being. Though his heart was repeatedly broken in grief, he lived well and he died well. One of his students said, 'How he strove to be like his Master, who was meek and lowly in heart.' Men who knew him ranked him alongside Augustine and John Calvin. But the keynote of his life is found in this message to his sons: 'Follow God fully without turning aside.'

Dabney's wife placed over his grave a granite monument with this inscription:

In unshaken loyalty of devotion to his friends, his country, and his religion, firm in misfortune, ever active in earnest endeavor, he labored all his life for what he loved, with a faith in good causes, that was ever one with his faith in God.

One day he and his sons will rise together from the ground to meet the Lord in the air. He will see with his own eyes the Saviour that he loves and his three boys. I hope to meet them and to stand with them, and with my own sons and daughter before the throne of heaven to worship the Son of God.

Where now is the love of God? He did not spare my dying child or come to the aid of my prayer. My child has been torn from my heart, to be carried out to the grave.

ABRAHAM KUYPER

. . . another also came and said, 'Your sons and daughters were eating and drinking wine in their oldest brother's house, and suddenly a great wind came . . . and struck the four corners of the house, and it fell on the young people, and they are dead' . . . Then Job arose, tore his robe, and shaved his head; and he fell to the ground and worshipped And he said, '. . . The LORD gave, and the LORD has taken away; blessed be the name of the LORD.' In all this Job did not sin nor charge God with wrong.

JOB 1:18-22

7

Not As I Will

Abraham Kuyper, the Dutch prime-minister and theologian, observed that there is an increase in the knowledge of God that comes when we ourselves 'will' what God ordains concerning us; when willingly we adapt ourselves to what he has determined for us according to his perfectly wise and good counsel; and when we accept everything that our lot in life brings us, not only without complaint and murmuring, but with the historic courage of faith. Often, however, one must travel over rough and painful terrain before coming to this knowledge of God.

In his book *To Be Near unto God,* Kuyper explains how our knowledge of God increases through adversity. He gives the example of a bereaved mother, who first knows God only in the context of pleasant times. For her, life and happiness really consist in the things she has and not in God himself. Then comes tragedy. Her world is forever changed, and she finds that God is not as she had dreamed him to be. In the end, though, she finds that it is not God who has changed, but it is she who has been transformed by the renewing of the mind. 'This happens', said Kuyper, 'again and again in life.' He writes:

A woman was most happy; hers was a pure delight in the possession of husband and child. An overwhelming sense of happiness found frequent expression in thanksgiving and praise. The love of her Father in heaven was so great. He made her so happy, her cup was full to overflowing. But things change. Serious illness breaks up the quiet and peace, and the child is snatched away by death. Now everything is gone. Now she cannot be comforted. Now her deeply wounded soul rises up in rebellion against God.

It has all been self-deception—misleading. No, God cannot be love. How could a God who is Love be so cruel as to cast her down from the heights of her great happiness into the depths of bereavement and grief? And in the bewilderment of affliction, words of despair and of defiant unbelief flow from her lips. 'Talk no more of God to me. Cruelty cannot love. There is no God.' So the break of happiness in life becomes the break of faith in the soul. She fancied that she knew God, and now that He appears different from what she had imagined, she gives up all faith. With her child she also lost her God. And what is left in the soul is but a burned-out hearth from which the last spark has been extinguished.

This makes you feel how hard the lesson is which, through the school of suffering, must make us increase in the knowledge of God. When for the first time in our life the cross with its full weight is laid upon our shoulders, the first effect is that it makes us numb and dazed and causes all knowledge of God to be lost.

The psalm of love was so beautiful, it glided into our soul so sweetly. A God who is only Love, love for us, in order to bless us, to make our life rich and glad—Oh, who would not willingly attain unto the knowledge of such a God?

In our life among men it is indeed glorious when love and nothing but love is shown us. And how rich, then, our heart feels in the possession of a God who causes only love, only streams of happiness and peace to flow out after us.

But now dawns the day of adversity, the day of trouble and disappointment, the day of sickness and grief. 'Where now is the love of God? He did not spare my dying child or come to the aid of my prayer. My child has been torn from my heart, to be carried out to the grave.'

And of course, in the end, this must bring it about, that we attain to another, a better knowledge of God, which explains His dealings with us. But at first what our heart feels is that we cannot square this with our God as we had imagined Him, as we had dreamed Him to be. The God we had, we lose, and then it costs so much bitter conflict of soul, before refined and purified in our knowledge of God, we grasp another, and now the only true God in the place thereof.

The first lesson consists in this, that in actual life, with our whole outward and inner existence, we give in to a higher decree, and bow before an All-power, against which we can do nothing. And this seems dreadful, but yet this very thing is the discovery of God as *God* in the reality of our experience.

As long as we have only just started on the way to the cross, we fancy ourselves the main object at stake; it is our happiness, our honor, our future — and God added in. According to our idea we are the center of things, and God is there to make us happy. The Father is for the sake of the child. And God's confessed Almightiness is solely and alone to serve our interest. This is an idea of God which is false through and through, which turns the order around and, taken in its real sense, makes self God, and God our servant.

From this false knowledge of God the cross removes all foundation. Cast down by your sorrow and grief, you become suddenly aware that this great God does not measure nor direct the course of things according to your desire; that in His plan there are other motives that operate entirely outside of your preferences. Then you must submit, you must bend. You stand before it in utter impotence, and from this selfsame heaven, in which thus far you saw nothing but the play of light and clouds, darkness now enters into your soul, the clap of thunder reverberates in your heart, and the flaming bolt of lightning fills you with dismay.

This is the discovery of God's reality, of His Majesty which utterly overwhelms you, of an Almightiness which absorbs within itself you and everything you call yours. And for the first time you feel what it is to confront the living God. Such is God. Now you know Him!

And then begins the new endeavor of the soul, to learn to understand this real God. Then begins the questioning, the guessing, the pondering, *why* this Almighty God should be the way He is and do the things He does. Then the troubled heart seeks an explanation. It seeks this in its guilt and sin. It seeks this in the after-effects of the past. It seeks this in the purpose for which the cross was laid upon us, and in the fruit which it shall bear in the unraveling of eternity. For a long time it still remains the endeavor of finding the explanation of God's doing solely and alone in *ourselves*.

Then the soul makes a still further advance. It abandons the theory of Job's friends and, like Job, receives the answer from God Himself out of the whirlwind. It now learns to understand how God's appointment covers all suns and stars, all hours and centuries, and causes all creatures to revolve themselves around Him, the Eternal One, as the one and only center; and, therefore, His counsel and plan are as high as heaven and consequently exceed our comprehension. It learns that, not the verification of His counsel, but the entering into the life of it, whether it be through joy, whether it be through sorrow, is our honor and the self-exaltation of our soul.

This breaks the passiveness that destroys our strength, and quickens again that which imparts heroic courage to drink the cup, to drink it willingly, and not let it be forced upon us. To will to drink, as Jesus willed to die on Golgotha—with a broken heart, to co-operate in God's work, and in this suffering co-operation with God, who slays us, to find eternal life.

The soul is thus like the sentinel who lets himself be shot down at his post and, in dying, enjoys the approving look of his general. And he rejoices therein, because he knows, and now sees, that the general, who ordered him to death, yet loved him.[1]

There is a great tension in Kuyper's story between appearance and reality. At first, there is the appearance of defeat as the woman's world is torn apart by the death of her child. God seemed farther away from her than when she was enjoying herself and her pleasant life. Yet what looked like ruin was, in reality, victory as the sovereign majesty of God burst through the darkness to illuminate the woman's heart. God was not tearing down; He was raising up. He was not moving away, but drawing near. This is Kuyper's point: In times of adversity and gloom, 'Draw near to God and he will draw near to you. Humble yourselves in the sight of the Lord, and he will lift you up' (*James* 4:8, 10).

[1] Abraham Kuyper, *To Be Near unto God*, trans. J. H. De Vries (New York: Macmillan, 1918).

Then Job answered the LORD *and said: 'I know that you can do everything, and that no purpose of yours can be withheld from you . . . I have heard of you by the hearing of the ear, but now my eye sees you.'*

JOB 42:1, 5

God had given me a son. God hath taken my little boy, but I have myriads of sons throughout the Christian world.

JOHN CALVIN

8

MORE TEARS

JOHN CALVIN

JOHN CALVIN was born in France during the summer of 1509. In the early 1530s Calvin became interested in the doctrines of the Protestant Reformation. He embraced the cause and worked to advance it in the city of Paris.

A great persecution borke out against the reformers in France. Calvin fled from Paris and eventually settled in the Swiss city of Geneva. There he worked tirelessly as a pastor and completed the final version of his celebrated *Institutes of the Christian Religion*. Many Protestant refugees, like John Knox, came from Scotland, England and other parts of Europe to study Christian doctrine and the life of the church in Geneva. As they later returned to their various homelands, Calvin's influence spread throughout Europe.

Calvin married a widow named Idalette, who already had two children. The happy couple had only one child of their own—a premature baby boy who died in infancy. In grief Calvin wrote to a friend:

> The Lord has certainly dealt a severe and bitter blow in the death of my infant son. But he is himself a Father, and knows best what is good for his children.

One of Calvin's adversaries taunted him about his loss. Calvin answered simply, 'God had given me a son. God hath taken my little boy, but I have myriads of sons throughout the Christian world.'

For Calvin, life consisted in more than just having physical descendants. No, for him, all of life was wrapped up in Jesus Christ and the raising up of faithful sons and daughters in the church. Christ was his chief love and highest place of refuge.

These thoughts overflowed into the following hymn written by Calvin:

> I greet Thee, who my sure Redeemer art,
> My only trust and Saviour of my heart,
> Who pain didst undergo for my poor sake:
> I pray Thee from our hearts all cares to take.
>
> Thou art the King of mercy and of grace,
> Reigning omnipotent in ev'ry place:
> So come, O King, and our whole being sway;
> Shine on us with the light of Thy pure day.

Thou art the Life, by which alone we live,
And all our substance and our strength receive;
O comfort us in death's approaching hour,
Strong-hearted then to face it by Thy pow'r.

Thou has the true and perfect gentleness,
No harshness hast Thou, and no bitterness;
O grant to us the grace we find in Thee,
That we may dwell in prfect unity.

Our hope is in no other save in Thee;
Our faith is built upon Thy promise free;
Come, give us peace, make us so strong and sure,
That we may conquerors be, and ills endure.[1]

In 1564 the beloved pastor of Geneva died. It is said that, next to Martin Luther, Calvin accomplished more for the reformation of the church than any other individual. In his last will, Calvin wrote,

> I confess to live and die in this faith which God has given me, inasmuch as I have no other hope or refuge than his predestination upon which my salvation is grounded. I embrace the grace which he has offered me in our Lord Jesus Christ, and accept the merits of his suffering and dying that through him all my sins are buried; and I humbly beg him to wash me and cleanse me with the

---

[1] *Strasburg Psalter*, 1545: tr. by Elizabeth Lee Smith (1817-98), altd.

blood of our great Redeemer, as it was shed for all poor sinners so that I, when I appear before his face, may bear his likeness.[2]

MATTHEW HENRY

I have been this day doing a work I never did before–burying a child. A sad day's work!

MATTHEW HENRY

Well-known and still loved to this day for his time-less commentary on the Bible, Matthew Henry was also a man most acquainted with sorrow. It is said that he was born prematurely and was so weak at birth that no-one expected him to live. When he was about five years old, he and his brother both had the measles. Matthew survived, but his older brother died.

At the age of twenty-five, the young minister and his wife, Katherine, were married and they lived in Chester, England, where Matthew pastored a church. But this pleasant scene, like many earthly ones, was of very short continuance.

Within a year and a half, Katherine was seized with smallpox while pregnant and died, though the child was spared.

[2] *Letters of John Calvin* (Edinburgh: Banner of Truth, 1980).

An intimate friend came to visit the house of mourning. Matthew Henry's first words to his friend, spoken with tears, were these:

> I know nothing could support me under such a loss as this, but the good hope I have that she is gone to heaven, and that in a little time I shall follow her there.

At the baptismal ceremony for the daughter (who was given the name, Katherine, in memory of her mother), Henry professed his Christian faith and said, 'I offer up my child to the great God, a plant out of a dry ground, desiring that she may be implanted into Christ.' Every heart of those who attended the sacrament was full, and few dry eyes were seen.

Under this severe affliction, God strengthened Henry's heart so that he pursued his pastoral work with his usual diligence. At length a kind providence repaired his loss, and he married a second time. Over the next twenty-two years, Henry had nine children, eight daughters and one son. Three of them died in infancy. Of his first loss, Henry wrote in his journal:

> I have been this day doing a work I never did before — burying a child. A sad day's work! But a good friend preached very seasonably and excellently, from Psalm 39:9, *I was dumb, I opened not my mouth, because it was You who did it.*

On the birth of his fourth child, Henry wrote, 'This child comes into a world of tears.' The child was taken away in death less than a year and a half later, and upon the occasion, Henry recorded these thoughts:

My desire is to be sensible of the affliction, and yet patient under it. It is a smarting rod; God calls my sins to remembrance—the coldness of my love, my abuse of spiritual comforts.

But he adds,

It is a rod in the hand of a Father. I desire to see a father's authority, who may do what he will; and a father's love, who will do what is best. We resign the soul of the child to Him that gave it.—I am in deaths often; Lord, teach me how to die daily.[3]

❦

GEORGE WHITEFIELD

At first, I was shaken, but looking up I recovered my strength . . .

GEORGE WHITEFIELD
[after the death of his first child]

To explain God's providence by His promise, and not

---

[3] Matthew Henry, *An Exposition of the Old and New Testaments*, Vol. 1 (New York: Robert Carter and Brothers, n. d.).

*His promise by His providence, I find is the only way
both to get and to keep our comforts.*

GEORGE WHITEFIELD

[after the death of his second child]

Like Bunyan before him, George Whitefield was a man committed to the doctrine of God's sovereignty in all issues of life, especially in the salvation of his chosen covenant people.

When the Church of England barred Whitefield from its pulpits in the late 1730's, he took to the open-air and preached the new birth and salvation in Christ to the common man. In the following years, he played a major part in the spiritual renewal of England and colonial America, a time known as the Great Awakening.

In the summer of 1742, news reached the itinerant preacher that his sister, Elizabeth, had died. To comfort his mother, Whitefield wrote to her,

Honoured Mother,

I rejoice to hear that you have been staying so long at my home. Blessed be God, that I have a house in which my honoured mother may stay. You are most welcome to anything my house affords, as long as you please. If it were necessary, indeed, rather go without myself, than you should lack anything. I will be highly pleased when I come and find you sitting in your youngest son's house. O that I may sit with you, in the house not made with hands, eternal in the heavens! Ere long, your death, honoured mother, will come. You must go there shortly and be seen no more. Your only daughter, I trust, is now in the paradise of God. I think I hear her say, 'Mother, come up here.' Jesus, I am sure, calls you in His word. May His Spirit enable you to say, 'Lord, lo I come!' My honoured mother, I am happier and happier every day. Jesus makes me exceedingly happy in Himself. If anyone should ask about me, please tell them, I am well both in body and soul, and desire them to help me praise free and sovereign grace. O that my dear, very honoured mother may be made an everlasting monument of it! How does my heart burn with love and duty to you. Gladly would I wash your aged feet, and lean upon your neck, and weep and pray 'till I could pray no more. With this I send you a thousand dutiful salutations, and ten thousand hearty and most humble thanks for all the pains you underwent in conceiving, bringing forth, nursing, bringing up, honoured mother,

> Your most unworthy,
> though most dutiful son,
> 'till death,
> G.W.[4]

Less than two years later, at age 29, Whitefield had a son, John, and he rashly proclaimed that his child would grow up to be a great preacher. But God had a more perfect plan for John.

[4] George Whitefield, *Letters* (Edinburgh: Banner of Truth, 1976).

The Whitefields were too poor to afford their place in London. Though it was then winter, Whitefield and his wife, Elizabeth, agreed that she and their four-month-old son would move to a cottage in Wales (with a planned stop along the way in Gloucester, at the old family inn which was being run by Whitefield's brother). Whitefield continued his preaching ministry and, as soon as his schedule allowed, he joined Elizabeth in Gloucester.

When he arrived at the inn, he learned that the child had become sick and died. In a letter, Whitefield told the story.

I immediately called on all to join in prayer, and I blessed the Father of mercies for giving me a son, though he was taken from me so soon. All joined in desiring that I would decline preaching till the child was buried; but I remembered a saying of good Mr Matthew Henry, 'that weeping must not hinder sowing', and therefore preached twice the next day, and also the day following; on the evening of which, just as I was closing my sermon, the bell struck for the funeral. At first, I was shaken, but looking up I recovered my strength, and then concluded with saying that 'all things work together for good to them that love God (Romans 8:28)', and this made me as willing to go out to my son's funeral, as to hear of his birth.

Our parting with him was solemn. We kneeled down, prayed and shed many tears. And then, as he died in the house where I was baptized, first took the Sacrament of the Lord's Table and first preached, I was comforted from that passage in the Book of Kings (2 Kings 4:18-37) which records the death [and resurrection] of the Shunammite's child and the woman's answer to the Prophet when he asked, 'Is it well with thee? Is it well with thy husband? Is it well with the child?' And she answered, 'It is well.'

Though disappointed of a living preacher by the death of my son, yet I hoped what happened before his birth, and since his death, has taught me such lessons, which may render his mistaken parent more cautious, more soberminded, and consequently more useful in his future labours to the church of God.[5]

Years later, Elizabeth was again 'expecting an hour of travail', but like her first, this child also died. In a letter to a close friend, Whitefield does not even mention this sorrow, but says, 'To explain God's providence by His promise, and not His promise by His providence, I find is the only way both to get and to keep our comforts.'[6]

When my own son was sick and dying, I remembered reading some years before about George Whitefield and his words about the death of his first child. I found the book, read the story again and was greatly comforted. This was the beginning of my journey on the 'old paths' and my search for other stories of Christian men and women of similar experiences, to draw strength from them (the end result is this book). To turn an often-used

[5] Ibid.
[6] Luke Tyerman, *The Life and Times of the Reverend George Whitefield*, Vol. 2 (London: Hodder and Stoughton, 1877).

phrase of Whitefield: These Christians 'go before, I follow, though with unequal steps'.

> *My life, my blood, I here present,*
> *If for Thy truth they may be spent,*
> *Fulfil Thy sov'reign counsel, Lord:*
> *Thy will be done! Thy Name ador'd!*
>
> *Give me Thy strength, O God of power,*
> *Then let winds blow, or thunders roar,*
> *Thy faithful witness will I be—*
> *'Tis fix'd! I can do all through Thee![7]*

GEORGE WHITEFIELD

JONATHAN EDWARDS

*Though you are at so great a distance from us, yet God
is everywhere. You are much out of the reach of our
care, but you are every moment in His hands.*

JONATHAN EDWARDS

A long with George Whitefield, another man inextri-
cably linked with the Great Awakening in America
was Jonathan Edwards, pastor of a congregational
church in Northampton, Massachusetts. In 1739, just
before the great revival, Whitefield wrote to Edwards

---

[7] George Whitefield, *Journals* (Edinburgh: Banner of Truth, 1989).

saying,

> I rejoice for the great things God has done for many
> souls in Northampton . . . Now is the gathering time.
> A winnowing time will shortly succeed. Persecution
> and the power of religion will always keep pace.
> Our Lord's word begins to be glorified in America.
> Many hearts gladly receive it. Oh, Rev Sir, it grieves
> me to see people, everywhere ready to perish for lack
> of knowledge. I care not what I suffer, so that some
> may be brought home to Christ . . . May the God of
> grace give you all peace and joy in believing! May
> he increase you more and more, both you and your
> children . . .
>
> > Your unworthy brother,
> > fellow labourer and servant
> > in our dear Lord,
> > G.W.[8]

In the spring of 1747, Edwards began a close friendship
with David Brainerd, a young missionary to the American
Indians.

Unfortunately, this friendship came to an end all too
soon. When Brainerd arrived in Northampton, he was already suffering from advanced tuberculosis. Edwards and
his family, especially Edwards' second daughter, Jerusha,
did their best to nurse Brainerd, but his health continued
to decline.

---

[8] Iain H. Murray, *Jonathan Edwards, A New Biography* (Edinburgh: Banner
of Truth, 1987)

On Sunday, October 4, 1747, Jerusha entered Brainerd's room. He looked upon her and said,

Dear Jerusha, are you willing to part with me?—I am quite willing to part with you. I am willing to part with all my friends. Though if I thought I should not see you and be happy with you in another world, I could not bear to part with you. But we shall spend a happy eternity together.

Brainerd died five days later, and Jerusha joined him in death the following winter. Of this sad event, her father wrote:

Since this [Brainerd's death], it has pleased a holy and sovereign God, to take away my dear child by death, on the 14 of February, next following, after a short illness, in the 18th year of her age. She was a person of much the same spirit with Brainerd. She had constantly taken care of and attended him in his sickness, for nineteen weeks before his death; devoting herself to it with great delight, because she looked on him as an eminent servant of Jesus Christ. In this time, he had much conversation with her on the things of religion; and, in his dying state, often expressed to us, her parents, his great satisfaction concerning her true piety, and his confidence that he should meet her in heaven, and his high opinion of her not only as a real Christian, but as a very eminent saint: one whose soul was uncommonly fed and entertained with things which pertain to the most spiritual, experimental, and distinguishing parts of religion: and one, who, by the temper of her mind, was fitted to deny herself for God, and to do good, beyond any young woman he knew. She had manifested a heart uncommonly devoted to God in the course of her life, many years before her death; and said on her death-bed, that she had not seen one minute, for several years, wherein she desired to live one minute longer, for the sake of any other good in life, but doing good, living to God, and doing what might be for his glory.[9]

Edwards buried Jerusha in a grave next to Brainerd's, and the family marked her gravestone with words from Psalm 17:15, 'I shall be satisfied, when I awake, with thy likeness.'

Some months later, but not so long that the pain of Jerusha's death would have faded, Jonathan Edwards wrote a touching letter to his daughter Mary while she was away from the family household.

Northampton,
July 26, 1749

To Miss Mary Edwards
My Dear Child,

You may well think it is natural for a parent to be concerned for a child at so great a distance, so far out of view, and so far out of the reach of communication;

[9] Sereno E. Dwight, *Memoirs of Jonathan Edwards* from *The Works of Jonathan Edwards* (Edinburgh: Banner of Truth, 1974).

where, if you should be taken with any dangerous sickness, that should end in death, you might probably be in your grave before we could hear of your danger. But yet, my greatest concern is not for your health, or earthly welfare, but for the good of your soul. Though you are at so great a distance from us, yet God is everywhere. You are much out of the reach of our care, but you are every moment in His hands. We have not the comfort of seeing you, but He sees you. His eye is always upon you. And if you may but live sensibly near to God, and have his gracious presence, it is no matter if you are far distant from us. I had rather you should remain hundreds of miles distant from us, and have God near to you by his Spirit, than to have you always with us, and live at a distance from God. And if the next news we should hear of you, should be of your death, though that would be very sad; yet, if at the same time we should receive such news concerning you, as should give us the best grounds to hope, that you had died in the Lord, how much more comfortable would this be, though we should have no opportunity to see you, or to take our leave of you in your sickness, than if we should be with you during all its progress, and have much opportunity to attend upon you, and talk and pray with you, and take an affectionate leave of you, and after all have reason to think, that you died without the grace and favor of God! It is comfortable to have the presence of earthly friends, especially in sickness, and on a death-bed; but the great thing is to have God our friend, and to be united to Christ, who can never die any more, and from whom our own death cannot separate us.

My desire and daily prayer is, that you may, if it may consist with the holy will of God, meet with God where you are, and have much of his divine influences on your heart, wherever you may be; and that, in God's due time, you may be reunited to us again, in all respects under the smiles of Heaven, and especially, in prosperous circumstances in your soul, and that you may find us all alive and well. But that is uncertain; for you know what a dying time it has been with us in this town, about this season of the year, in years past. There is not much sickness prevailing among us as yet, but we fear whether mortal sickness is not now beginning. Yesterday, the only remaining son of Mr. C____ died with a fever, and is to be buried today. May God fit us all for his will!

I hope that you will maintain a strict and constant watch over yourself, against all temptations, that you do not forsake and forget God, and particularly, that you do not grow slack in private religious devotion. Retire often from this vain world, from all its bubbles and empty shadows, and vain amusements, and talk with God alone; and seek effectually for that divine grace and comfort, the least drop of which is worth more than all the riches, gaiety, pleasures, and entertainments of the whole world . . .

We are all, through the Divine goodness, in a tolerable state of health . . . But the whole family has indeed much to put us in mind, and make us sensible, of our dependence on the care and kindness of God, and of the vanity of all human dependencies; and we are very loudly called upon to seek his face, to trust in him, and walk closely with him. Commending you to the care and special favor of our heavenly Father, I am Your very affectionate father,

Jonathan Edwards[10]

This is the kind of letter that every Christian father and mother should write to their children at least once in life, and the kind of letter we hope our children will take to heart, for we have no greater joy than to hear that our children are walking in the truth.

SELINA HASTINGS, THE COUNTESS OF HUNTINGDON

The cloud would be so dark did I not see my Lord in it; this 'must needs be' heaviness may endure for a night but 'joy comes in the morning'.

SELINA HASTINGS

Lament if you please, but Glory, glory, glory be to God.

JOHN BERRIDGE

[10] Ibid.

Selina Hastings, The Countess of Huntingdon, was a close friend of Charles Wesley and George White-field. She appointed Whitefield as her chaplain, and used her wealth and position in life, not only to gener-ously support Whitefield's ministry but also to bring the gospel of Christ to the ranks of the nobility and royalty of her times.

In April 1743, Selina's ten-year old son, Ferdinando died of smallpox while she was away in Bristol, England. 'Ferdy' was buried in London's Westminister Abbey, and Selina grieved deeply for him. She wrote of her grief to Charles Wesley:

> Nature says often O! My son, my son! Very pleasant hast thou been, but all the happiness that yet remains in the other five [remaining children] I have freely offered rather than one single thought should arise in my heart in the course of this trial contrary to the will of God, and I have yet confidence that in this thing I shall be kept.[11]

Selina's grief was deepened because she was not with her son when he died. She told her husband,

> Poor Ferdy has been the subject of my dreams many nights—this last particularly for no creature was ever so unhappy about another having to go through his whole sickness and death [alone]. It has made such an

[11] Faith Cook, *Selina, Countess of Huntingdon* (Edinburgh: Banner of Truth, 2001). All of the quotations in this part about Selina Hastings come from Cook's work.

impression on me that in the midst of the most remote thoughts it jumps in and damps my spirit.

Added to all this, three of her other children were also sick, and Selina naturally feared that they, too, might fall to smallpox. Here, though, she was enabled to walk by faith, and not take counsel of her fears.

Again, to her husband she wrote:

Nothing is too hard for the love and mercy of God and therefore I will hope that he will (as he easily can) raise them up again . . . [But] sure I am that all is wise and best that happens. I trust in his power to keep my heart from rebelling against him. And let us, my dear, dear soul, submit all to the divine will. He knows what is best.

Later that year, five days before Christmas, the unthinkable happened, and Selina's son, George, died of smallpox before reaching his fourteenth birthday. Yet, in the midst of these days of sorrow, and though Selina was still a young Christian, she was able to say to Charles Wesley,

The cloud would be so dark did I not see my Lord in it; this 'must needs be' heaviness may endure for a night but 'joy comes in the morning'.

Fifteen years later grief would again visit Selina when her son, Henry, fell ill. With his health failing, and also receiving the news of the death of her new-born grandchild, Selina wrote about both events to Wesley. In her letter, which also mentions the health of her youngest daughter, who was also named Selina, the Countess said:

My very kind Friend,

Your letters were a great comfort to me . . . My sorrows have taken such hold upon me that I was not able to look up—from whence cometh my help? . . . Yet I would not have had one sigh or tear less for the friendship of the world . . . My poor son's sight grows worse . . . and I am in the midst of much I wish otherwise . . . but his heart and spirit conquered by grace is my one wish about him now. O could this be given me my heart would re-joice in the midst of my present grief about him . . . My daughter [Elizabeth] has been happily brought through the birth of a son who lived just to suffer much—a few hours and then died. Lady Selina is, I praise God, well. You see how I speak of blessings with thankfulness to you as I would my sorrows with patience.

Shortly before Henry's death, Selina again confided in Charles Wesley, simply saying 'All things work together for good and in this blind hope, under the most unintel-ligible events, I rest secure, and am determined to make no explanations for myself.' After Henry's death, Selina wrote once more to Charles:

I shall surprise you more when I tell you my testimony of my dear child's happiness was not, nor is not, transient. No, I see him, I feel him in that inseparable union with

God that neither time, place or frame or temper alters; and yet when the sensations of the joy in that union abates, his death, his manner of death, his long and sore affliction, is felt with sensibility that nothing but the like feeling can describe.

With Henry's passing, Selina had buried her husband and three of their six children.

One would think that a mother could not bear any more griefs, but death would visit the Countess of Huntingdon for a fourth child, her daughter, Lady Selina. To William Romaine, the author of *The Life, Walk and Triumph of Faith*, Selina wrote:

It pleased our dear God and only Saviour to take from me, May 12, 1763, at three quarters after four in the morning, my dearest, my altogether lovely child and daughter, Lady Selina Hastings, the desire of my eyes and continual pleasure of my heart . . . She often desired me to pray by her, and with great earnestness accompanied me . . . She often called on the Lord Jesus to have mercy on her, and complained of her impatience, though no-one ever heard a complaint pass her lips, though her sufferings were very great . . . During the last four days, these sentences at times fell from her, 'Jesus, teach me! — Jesus, wash me! — cleanse me, and purify me!' . . . Another time she said, 'I am happy as my heart can desire to be.' The day before her death, I came to her and asked her if she knew me. She said, 'My dear mother!' I then asked her if her heart was happy? She said, '. . . I am happy, very, very happy!' . . . She often said, to be resigned to God's will was all, and that she had no hope of salvation but in the mercy of Jesus Christ alone.

Following this last ordeal, Selina received many letters of consolation. Lord Dartmouth wrote saying:

Little did we imagine when we had the pleasure of seeing her so lately in London that she was so near the confines of the eternal world. But we know not what a day or a night may bring forth. Though nature must feel the loss of such a darling object, now must your Ladyship's grief be mingled with joyful satisfaction . . . that the noble evidence she gave of the grace and hope of the Gospel, and the loving-kindness and mercy of the Saviour manifested in her dying moments. Oh, my dear Madam, Lady Selina is now singing the praises of redeeming love before the throne of God and of the Lamb.

Another friend wrote:

Blessed be God for giving us the unspeakable satisfaction to see Lady Selina safely landed, out of the reach of vanity. This is mercy rejoicing over judgment of a truth . . . Come, my Lady, let us travel on, sticking close to our heavenly Guide; let us keep a hold of the hem of his garment by firmly believing the arms of his wise providence and everlasting love are underneath us; let us hasten to our friends in light . . . Lord Jesus, come quickly, and let us all be lost together in thy love and praise.

So, it has been written of the Countess that she began to 'travel on'. How did she do it? Faith Cook, in her biography of Selina, has observed that

> The antidote to her sorrow lay not so much in putting her bereavement behind her, as in focusing on the delight that Selina was now experiencing in a better world and in throwing her energies once more into the work of God.[12]

Please do not miss this keen observation. It is a lesson the grieving sojourner must learn to move forward.

The story of Selina Hastings is a wonderful testimony to the strength of a woman to go through the valley of weeping. I saw such strength firsthand, watching my wife 'travel on' after the death of our son, knowing that John Cameron was now in a better place and helping parents who have sick and dying children, as well as those having the ongoing challenges of raising children with disabilities. Still, we must recognize that we are all 'weak vessels' in need of much grace in times of grief, and, whether man or woman, young or old, we all persevere and move forward by the grace of the God, who is no respecter of persons. He gives comfort to all without distinction.

[12] Ibid.

Lemuel Haynes

*The meeting of parents and children at the judgment is
a truly affecting thought, which, since the decease of
my own child, I most sensibly realize.*

Lemuel Haynes

Born in 1753, Lemuel Haynes was abandoned by his
parents when he was only five months old, but in the providence of God, he became an indentured servant of David
Rose, whom Haynes called 'a man of singular piety', and
there he found a loving home. Mrs Rose especially treated
Lemuel as one of her own children.

Upon reaching manhood and the end of his indentured
service, Lemuel Haynes volunteered as a Minuteman and
later joined the Continental Army. Haynes was an American patriot; he was also a 'son of Africa'.

Early on, young Lemuel 'got his education in the
chimney corner'. He was 'a determined, self-taught
student who poured over Scripture until he could repeat
from memory most of the texts dealing with the doctrines of grace.'[13] He benefitted from his early training,
but 'the works of Jonathan Edwards, George White-

---

[13] Helen MacLam, 'Introduction: Black Puritan on the Northern Frontier',
in *Black Preacher to White America: The Collected Writings of Lemuel
Haynes, 1774–1833* (New York: Carlson, 1990), as quoted by Thabiti M.
Anyabwile, *The Faithful Preacher: Recapturing the Vision of Three
Pioneering African-American Pastors* (Wheaton: Crossway Books, 2007).

field, and Philip Doddridge influenced him the most.'[14] He eventually received formal ministerial training, and 'later became the first African-American ordained by any religious body in America.'[15] In his preaching, Haynes adopted the same principles as Edwards and Whitefield respecting the operations of the Holy Spirit. He was distinguished for 'directness and unction . . . calculated to quicken the believer in his course, to rouse the impenitent sinner from his dangerous slumber, and to guide him to the Lamb of God as the only hope of salvation.'[16]

Haynes married Elizabeth Babbit. Together they had ten children, and together they experienced the death of one of those children—a daughter. This experience is retold by Haynes' biographer, T. M. Cooley.

> His second daughter had been afflicted with severe and wasting disease, which neither care nor medicine could relieve. For months all hopes of her recovery had been relinquished, and she was perceptively drawing near the close of life. But great mercy was mingled with the affliction. By her marked resignation and patience, she was giving evidence of being one of God's adopted children. One morning in particular, having called her father into her chamber, she spoke of wonderful joy and light which had broken in upon her mind. The Savior appeared exceedingly precious

[14] Thabiti M. Anyabwile, *The Faithful Preacher*.
[15] Ibid.
[16] Timothy M. Cooley, *Sketches of the Life and Character of the Rev. Lemuel Haynes* (Harper & Brothers, 1837; repr. New York: Negro Universities Press, 1969).

and altogether lovely. It was a memorable season, and filled the heart of her revered father with great consolation.

On the day before her death, Mr Haynes went out to attend a funeral and requested prayers in her behalf. She was now sinking rapidly. During his absence she became speechless, and seemed to be dying. On his return, as he approached her bed, she knew him, and revived. He then informed her that prayers had been offered for her at the meeting, at which she seemed well pleased. He talked long and faithfully with her, imparting consolation, praying her to put her whole trust in the merits of the Savior, and receiving from her dying lips assurance that Christ was her 'all'. The following morning she died, 'fallen asleep in Jesus'. The next day being the Sabbath, like David in his affliction, 'he came into the house of the Lord and worshiped', being joined by his family.

At his daughter's funeral service, Haynes gave out a hymn of Isaac Watts—

> *Not from the dust affliction grows,*
> *Nor troubles rise by chance,*
> *Yet we are born to cares and woes,*
> *A sad inheritance.*

> *As sparks break out from burning coals,*
> *And still are upward borne,*
> *So grief is rooted in our souls,*
> *And man grows up to mourn.*

Yet with my God I leave my cause,
And trust His promised grace;
He rules me by His well-known laws
Of love and righteousness.

Not all the pains that e'er I bore
Shall spoil my future peace,
For death and hell can do no more
Than what my Father please.

Throughout the painful trial, he showed great calmness and Christian resignation. It proved to be a sanctified affliction. The daughter was thus taken away and called home, a pioneer to that world where her father was soon to follow. And so was the Lord preparing his faithful servant to glorify him by his dying behavior. Scarcely would he allude to his daughter's decease without exclaiming, 'Oh, that I had been more faithful.'[17]

There is a remarkable account of a meeting between Haynes and a young lady who, deeply convicted of sin, did not understand her obligation towards God. The interview was short, but made its impression on the woman:

Question. 'Young woman! do you expect to go home tonight?'
Answer. 'Yes, sir.'
Question. 'How do you expect to get there?'
Answer. 'I expect to walk.'
Question. 'How will you walk? . . . I can tell you how

[17] Ibid.

you'll walk. You'll put one foot before t'other—that's the way you'll get home, if the Lord pleases. And that's the way to get to heaven—you must put one foot before t'other, and the Lord will take care of you. It is he who is calling you by his Spirit—and he calls you not to wait for him to carry you, but to follow him;—and then you have his promise that he will guide you by his counsels. But he will not carry you to heaven without you walking, any more than he will carry you home tonight while you sit there. You must put one foot before the other, and set out.[18]

There is application here for the grieving sojourner: God will bring you to a place of comfort, but you must follow him. The steep hill of grief may be scaled one step at a time. God will carry you up that hill, but you must also follow him, walking by faith and not by sight.

[18] Ibid.

Frederick Douglass

My darling sister is now an angel. Annie has gone to Him whose love is the same for the black as the white.

Rosetta Douglass

Frederick Douglass was born a slave; he died a free man. In his rise 'up from slavery', Douglass became one of the most important and influential men in American history and in that great struggle to abolish the horrific trade.

To arise out of bondage and live free among men is one thing. It is a wholly different thing to be a free man, spiritually.

Yet, I believe we read of both aspects of Douglass' freedom in his autobiographical work, *My Bondage and My Freedom*. In his chapter entitled, 'Religious Nature Awakened', Douglass describes the emancipation of the soul, which no human master can keep in chains and shackles, though he claims the body as own personal property:

> Previous to my contemplation of the anti-slavery movement, and its probable results, my mind had been seriously awakened to the subject of religion. I was not more than thirteen years old, when I felt the need of God, as a father and protector. My religious nature was awakened by the preaching of a white Methodist

minister, named Hanson. He thought that all men, great and small, bond and free, were sinners in the sight of God; that they were, by nature, rebels against His government; and that they must repent of their sins, and be reconciled to God, through Christ. I cannot say that I had a very distinct notion of what was required of me; but one thing I knew very well—I was wretched, and had no means of making myself otherwise. Moreover, I knew that I could pray for light. I consulted a good colored man, named Charles Johnson; and, in tones of holy affection, he told me to pray, and what to pray for. I was, for weeks, a poor, broken-hearted mourner, traveling through the darkness and misery of doubts and fears. I finally found that change of heart which comes by 'casting all one's care' upon God, and by having faith in Jesus Christ, as the Redeemer, Friend, and Savior of those who diligently seek Him.

After this, I saw the world in a new light. I seemed to live in a new world, surrounded by new objects, and to be animated by new hopes and desires. I loved all mankind—slaveholders not excepted; though I abhorred slavery more than ever. My great concern was, now, to have the world converted. The desire for knowledge increased, and especially did I want a thorough acquaintance with the contents of the Bible. I have gathered scattered pages from this holy book, from the filthy street gutters of Baltimore, and washed and dried them, that in the moments of my leisure, I might get a word or two of wisdom from them . . . I am careful to state these facts, that the reader may be able to form an idea of the precise influences which had to do with shaping and directing my mind.[19]

After reading these words of Douglass, it is hard not to think of the words of Psalm 107, 'Some sat in darkness and in the shadow of death, prisoners in affliction and in irons . . . Then they cried to the LORD in their trouble, and he delivered them from their distress. He brought them out of darkness and the shadow of death, and burst their bonds apart. Let them thank the LORD for his steadfast love . . .'

As Douglass grew into manhood, so grew his desire to escape the tyranny of slavery. With others of similar desires, he would often sing hymns about reaching a land of freedom and safety:

> *O Canaan, sweet Canaan,*
> *I am bound for the land of Canaan.*

But Douglass said that he and the others sang of something more than a hope of reaching heaven. 'We meant to reach the north—and the north was our Canaan.' Another favorite hymn was

> *I thought I heard them say,*
> *There were lions in the way,*
> *I don't expect to stay*
> *Much longer here.*

[19] Frederick Douglass, *My Bondage and My Freedom* (New York: Penguin Classics, 1855, repr. 2003).

Run to Jesus — shun the danger —
I don't expect to stay
Much longer here.

It, too, had a double meaning. Said Douglass,

In the lips of some, it meant the expectation of a speedy summons to a world of spirits; but in the lips of our company, it simply meant, a speedy pilgrimage toward a free state, and deliverance from all the evils and dangers of slavery.

Frederick Douglass eventually made his escape, and later, through the gifts of some generous friends, purchased his freedom from his former master. He was then, both in the eyes of God and men, a free man; but he would always carry with him the indelible marks of the slave life which he so well describes in his memoirs. In one particularly descriptive narrative, Douglass reflected on how the slaves would go to through the woods to the great plantation farm house on allowance day:

While on their way, they would make the dense old woods, for miles around, reverberate with their wild notes. These were not always merry because they were wild. On the contrary, they were mostly of a plaintive cast, and told a tale of grief and sorrow. In the most boisterous outbursts of rapturous sentiment, there was ever a tinge of deep melancholy . . . I have sometimes thought, that the mere hearing of those songs would do more to impress truly spiritual-

minded men and women with the soul-crushing and
death-dealing character of slavery, than the reading
of whole volumes of its mere physical cruelties. They
speak to the heart and to the soul of the thoughtful.
I cannot better express my sense of them now, than
ten years ago, when, in sketching my life, I thus spoke
of this feature of my plantation experience: I did not,
when a slave, understand the deep meanings of those
rude, and apparently incoherent songs. I was myself
within the circle, so that I neither saw or heard as
those without might see and hear. They told a tale
which was then altogether beyond my feeble comprehension; they were tones, loud, long and deep,
breathing the prayer and complaint of souls boiling
over with the bitterest anguish. Every tone was a
testimony against slavery, and a prayer to God for
deliverance from chains. The hearing of those wild
notes always depressed my spirits, and filled my heart
with ineffable sadness. The mere recurrence, even
now, afflicts my spirit, and while I am writing these
lines, my tears are falling. To those songs I trace my
first glimmering conceptions of the dehumanizing
character of slavery. I can never get rid of that con-
ception. Those songs still follow me, to deepen my
hatred of slavery, and quicken my sympathies for my
brethren in bonds. If any one wishes to be impressed
with a sense of the soul-killing power of slavery, let
him go to . . . [the] plantation, and, on allowance day,
place himself in the deep, pine woods, and there let

him, in silence, thoughtfully analyze the sounds that shall pass through the chambers of his soul, and if he is not thus impressed, it will only be because 'there is no flesh in his hardened heart.'

Douglass also said, 'I have never heard any songs like those anywhere since I left slavery, except when in Ireland. There I heard the same wailing notes, and was much affected by them. It was during the famine of 1845-6.'

People died by the hundreds of thousands during these years of the Irish potato famine; and it is a significant that Douglass, himself, would equate the songs of the slave with the songs of the bereaved. In the spring of 1860, these two songs would intersect in the life of Frederick Douglass.

Annie Douglass was the youngest of the five Douglass children. Her father called her 'the light and life of my house',[20] and when she died at the age of ten, Douglass admitted that he was 'deeply distressed by this bereavement'.[21] The fact that Douglass was in England at the time of his daughter's death only added to his distress. 'We heard from dear father last week', Rosetta (Douglass' first-born) told her sister, Harriet, 'and his grief was great.'

Letters of condolences from family members and others began to arrive at the Douglass household. One individual wrote to say,

---

[20] Frederick Douglass, *Life and Times of Frederick Douglass, Written by Himself* (1882, The Online Library of Liberty at oll.libertyfund.org).
[21] Ibid.

We deeply sympathize with you and your family in your late affliction. We felt that the blow would fall heavily upon you in a foreign land. 'Tis the Lord only that can soften such afflictions and to him we must go with our burdens.[22]

Sadly, no letters of Frederick Douglass about Annie's death are known to survive, but perhaps Rosetta spoke for the entire Douglass family when she wrote to Harriet saying, 'My darling sister is now an angel.' More than that, Rosetta claimed to take comfort in the thought that 'Annie has gone to Him whose love is the same for the black as the white.'[23]

George Müller

My soul laid hold in faith on that word, 'Of such is the kingdom of Heaven' . . . my soul rejoiced instead of mourning.

George Müller

Nothing is more marked in George Müller, to the very day of his death, than this, that he so looked to God and leaned on God that he felt himself to be nothing,

[22] Source: Library of Congress: http://memory.loc.gov/mss/mfd/03/03011/0003d.gif
[23] William S. McFeely, *Frederick Douglass* (New York: W. W. Norton & Company, 1991).

and God everything. He sought to be always and in all things surrendered as a passive tool to the will and hand of the Master Workman.

A. T. PIERSON

George Müller is best known for his orphanage, which he opened as a demonstration that God is sovereign, that he cares and provides for his people, and that he continues to be a Father to the fatherless. It is said that Müller never made a public plea for funds, but prayerfully trusted in God to supply the daily needs of the children. Müller died in 1898; the work at the orphanage which he began continues to this day.

When Müller was 26, his wife, Mary, gave birth to a stillborn baby. Mary remained seriously ill for several more weeks. Of this event, biographer A. T. Pierson said that Müller felt remorse for not having given more serious thought of the peril of child-birth, so as to pray more earnestly for his wife. He had not rejoiced in the prospect of parenthood as a blessing, but rather as a burden and hindrance in doing the Lord's work. Pierson added, 'God used this severe lesson for permanent blessing to George Müller by showing him how open his heart was to the subtle power of selfishness and carnality and to teach him the sacredness of marital life and parental responsibility.'

Müller and his wife later had a little girl and named her Lydia. Then they suffered the loss of another child, an infant son, Elijah, at age 15 months. This sad event followed just four days after Mary's father had died. Grandfather and grandson were laid in one grave. Müller wrote:

> When the Lord took from me a beloved infant, my soul was at peace, perfectly at peace; I could only weep tears of joy when I did weep. And why? Because my soul laid hold in faith on that word, 'Of such is the kingdom of Heaven' (Matt. 19:14). Believing in this word as I did, my soul rejoiced, instead of mourning, that my beloved infant was far happier with the Lord than with me.[24]

FANNY J. CROSBY

Hold Thou my hand; the way is dark before me
Without the sunlight of Thy face divine.

FANNY CROSBY

Frances ('Fanny') Crosby was one of the most popular American hymn writers. In her lifetime she wrote over 9,000 hymns, many of which, like 'Blessed Assurance' and 'Pass Me Not O Gentle Saviour', continue to grace our worship services to this day. As one would expect, so many of her hymns were borne out of

[24] A. T. Pierson, *George Müller of Bristol and His Witness to a Prayer-Hearing God* (Old Tappan, N. J.: Fleming H. Revell, 1899).

her own personal experiences. For example, a favourite hymn of her day was 'Hold Thou My Hand', which she wrote during a time of a time of despair—

Hold Thou my hand; so weak I am, and helpless,
I dare not take one step without Thy aid;
Hold Thou my hand, for then, O loving Saviour,
No dread of ill shall make my soul afraid.

Hold Thou my hand, and closer, closer draw me
To Thy dear self–my hope, my joy, my all;
Hold Thou my hand, lest haply I should wander,
And, missing Thee, my trembling feet should fall.

Hold Thou my hand; the way is dark before me
Without the sunlight of Thy face divine;
But when by faith I catch its radiant glory,
What heights of joy, what rapturous songs are mine![25]

Mrs Charles Spurgeon (then a widow) was so moved by this hymn that she wrote Crosby a note thanking her for the comforting and uplifting words. What makes this hymn, and especially the words, 'Hold Thou my hand; the way is dark before me', all the more remarkable and poignant is that Crosby had been blind since her infancy.

Fanny Crosby spent some of her younger years as a student at the Institution for the Blind in Oswego, New York. There she met another student, Alexander Van

---

[25] Fanny J. Crosby, as quoted by Edith L. Blumhofer, *Her Heart Can See: The Life and Hymns of Fanny J. Crosby* (Grand Rapids: Eerdmans, 2005).

Alstyne. A decade later, they were married, and together they had one child. Sadly, their child did not long survive. Crosby did not speak much about this time in her life, though late in life she said, 'the angels came down and took our infant up to God and to His throne.'[26] We can hear these words echoing in Crosby's hymn, 'Safe in the Arms of Jesus'—

> *Safe in the arms of Jesus,*
> *safe on his gentle breast,*
> *There by his love o'er shaded,*
> *sweetly my soul shall rest.*
> *Hark! 'tis the voice of angels,*
> *borne in a song to me*
> *Over fields of glory, over the jasper sea.*
> *Safe in the arms of Jesus,*
> *safe on his gentle breast,*
> *There by his love o'er shaded,*
> *sweetly my soul shall rest.*[27]

Fanny Crosby died shortly before her 95th birthday. The night before her death, as one of her last acts, she wrote a letter to comfort another family who had recently experienced the death of a child. Appropriately, the stone that marked Crosby's grave said simply, 'She hath done what she could.' What a fitting epitaph for us to contemplate about ourselves as we reach now the final part of

[26] Blumhofer, *Her Heart Can See.*
[27] Fanny J. Crosby, in *Trinity Hymnal* (Philadelphia: Great Christian Publications, 1961).

the sojourner's way through grief and find in it the way to glory.

Part Three

The Path to Glory

For I consider that the sufferings of this present time are not worthy to be compared with the glory which shall be revealed in us.

THE APOSTLE PAUL (*Rom.* 8:18)

Wherever men suffer, there will we be to comfort . . . Self-sacrifice means not indifference to our times and our fellows, it means absorption in them. It means forgetfulness of self in others. It means not that we should live one life, but a thousand lives—binding ourselves to a thousand souls by the filaments of so loving a sympathy that their lives become ours.

BENJAMIN B. WARFIELD

A mark of genuine Christianity is perseverance. Many trials may encompass believers, but they are kept by the power of God through faith. They have hope in the midst of adversity. They have been comforted by the living God, and this comfort tends to spill over into the lives of other hurting people. Sometimes we comfort others with a hand on the shoulder, a silent embrace, our tears mixing with theirs. Other times comforting words are shared. In every case it means taking our eyes off ourselves and looking outward to help others. It means, in the words of Benjamin Warfield, 'imitating the Incarnation' in self-sacrifice. Warfield wrote:

> Self-sacrifice brought Christ into the world. And self-sacrifice will lead us, His followers, not away from, but into the midst of men. Wherever men suffer, there will we be to comfort. Wherever men strive, there will we be to help. Wherever men fail, there will we be to uplift. Self-sacrifice means not indifference to our times and our fellows, it means absorption in them. It means forgetfulness of self in others. It means not that we should live one life, but a thousand lives—binding ourselves to a thousand souls by the filaments of so loving a sympathy

that their lives become ours. Only when we humbly walk this path, seeking truly in it not our own things but those of others, we shall find the promise true, that he who loses his life shall find it. Only when, like Christ, and in loving obedience to His call and example, we take no account of ourselves, but freely give ourselves to others, we shall find, each in his measure, the saying true of himself also: 'Wherefore also God hath highly exalted him.' The path of self-sacrifice is the path to glory.[1]

One of the foremost examples of a grieving parent walking on the path to glory is Robert Dabney. As we have already seen, he was deeply hurt by the loss of three small boys. Still he was willing to become a 'supporting parent' by meeting in person with another family, sharing in the pain and emotions of the moment and offering comforting words and prayers. To meet face to face is a fine way to encourage another person. A phone call can be just as helpful. Better still is a letter, for it is a long-lasting token of your concern for another.

One such letter was written by John Owen, a contemporary of John Bunyan. The two men knew one another; in fact, Owen helped Bunyan gain his release from prison. Though they held a common Christian faith, Owen and Bunyan were from opposite ends of the social spectrum. Bunyan was a poor, uneducated tinker. Owen was an Oxford graduate who preached before the king of England. But Owen greatly admired Bunyan. He would

---

[1] B. B. Warfield, *The Person and Work of Christ* (Philadelphia: Presbyterian and Reformed Publishing, 1950).

frequently hear Bunyan preach, which led Charles II to express his astonishment that a man of Owen's learning would listen to a tinker preach. It is said that Owen answered the king saying, 'Had I the tinker's abilities, please Your Majesty, I would gladly relinquish my learning.'

Not only did Owen and Bunyan become towering figures in England, being known for their faithful preaching and writing, their lives were also intertwined by the common experience of losing a child. Through his first marriage, Owen had eleven children, all of whom died young, except one daughter. What can compare to the lost love of ten children? For Owen, the love of God to us, in Christ, was better.

Having buried so many of his own children, Owen was well qualified to minister comfort to other grieving parents. He once poured out his heart in a sympathizing letter to a woman in his congregation. This letter has been providentially preserved for over three hundred years so that we too may draw comfort from it.

To Lady Hartopp,

Every work of God is good; the Holy One in the midst of us will do no iniquity; and all things shall work together for good unto them that love him; even those things which at present are not joyous, but grievous; only his time is to be waited for, and his way submitted unto, that we seem not to be displeased in our hearts, for he is Lord over us.

Your dear infant is in the eternal enjoyment of the

fruits of all our prayers, for the covenant of God is ordered in all things and sure. We shall go to her; she shall not return to us. She is happy in this above us, being born to move you to faith and patience and to glorify God's grace in her eternal blessedness.

My trouble would be great because of my absence from you at this time, were it not for knowing that this is also the Lord's doing. But I will beg of God for you both, that you may not faint in this day of trial, that you may clearly see all the spiritual and temporal mercies provided to you (none of which we deserve) so that the sorrow of the world would not overwhelm your hearts. God, in Christ, will be better to you than ten children, and he will preserve your family and add to it for his glory and your comfort. Shall I say, 'be cheerful'? I know I may. God help you to honour, grace and mercy. My heart is with you, my prayers shall be for you, and I am,

Dear Madam,
Your most affectionate friend,
and unworthy pastor,
J. Owen[2]

[2] John Owen, *The Works of John Owen*, Vol. 1 (London: Banner of Truth, 1965) pp. cxvi-cxvii.

My wife and I have kept all the letters that were written to us about John Cameron. All of the notes expressed sympathy. A few, however, touched my heart with special condolences. From Philadelphia we received kind words from Dr James Montgomery Boice, the late pastor of Tenth Presbyterian Church, who wrote:

> It was sad for me to get your note and learn that your infant son John died last month. I am sure the Lord has shown you many great mercies in these days, among them your being able to hold and commend him to the Lord as he died. Still I know how painful the time must have been and will be praying that God will give you a full measure of that divine peace that passes all understanding. I know that good things have already come from your suffering, and I will pray that you will see many more positive blessings in the days to come.

The most touching and instructive letter sent to us came from our own pastor. Though he did not mean it for publication, I hope he will forgive me for sharing here the wisdom and devotion that was displayed in his note to us. His letter simply said:

> I just wanted to remind you that all of us are united with you in prayer and spirit as you go through this trial of your faith.
>
> More importantly, Christ is with you, and the Spirit is interceding before the Father. God's grace is sufficient. We know, in the mystery of His providence, that all is for His glory and the edification of the body of Christ.

These truths are 'larger' than life—your life and the life of your baby. In the glories of the Kingdom yet to be revealed, we will know why.

Please remember that you are not alone. The church here, where we worship, and the church before the living God in the heavenlies is 'one' with you.

In your sadness, take comfort in God's infinite wisdom and sovereignty.

***

These two men continued the tradition and art of letter-writing that characterized so many of the pastors of bygone days. We ought to emulate them by writing a comforting note now and then to encourage others around us who seem to be hurting under the weight of life's distresses. It is a good way to give something of ourselves to others.

There is another important aspect of their notes that must not be overlooked. Both letters mention prayer. We should never forget the importance of intercessory prayer. It is a means by which God turns the circumstances of our distress into deliverance. 'For I know', Paul wrote from prison, 'that this will turn out for my deliverance through your prayer and the supply of the Spirit of Jesus Christ' (*Phil.* 1:19).

If 'binding ourselves' to others means anything at all, it surely means spending time in prayer for their needs. Every journey begins with one step. Prayer is a good step—if not the first step—along the path of self-sacrifice that leads from grief to glory.

> *Blessed be the God and Father of our Lord Jesus Christ, the Father of mercies and God of all comfort, who comforts us in all our tribulation, that we may be able to comfort those who are in any trouble, with the comfort with which we ourselves are comforted by God.*

2 CORINTHIANS 1:3-4

Your Lord may gather His roses whenever He pleases . . . You are taught to know and adore His sovereignty which He exercises over you, which yet is made radiant with mercy. The child hath but changed a bed in the garden, and is planted up higher, nearer the sun, where he shall thrive.

SAMUEL RUTHERFORD

9

SLEEPING IN THE BOSOM
OF THE ALMIGHTY

Samuel Rutherford was a Scottish pastor and theologian. For a time he was banished to prison for writing a defence of God's sovereign grace in saving sinners. There he wrote to a friend and said, 'My prison is a palace to me. I charge you in the name of God, I charge you to believe. Fear not the sons of men. Die believing. Stand for the truth of the gospel.'

Rutherford was restored to his pastoral work and was later sent to London as one of the Scottish Commissioners to the Westminster Aseembly. This Assembly drew up the the historic *Westminster Confession of Faith*. After Oliver Cromwell's period in power and following the restoration of Charles II to the throne of England, Rutherford again came under persecution. It is reported that when Charles saw Rutherford's book *Lex Rex (The Law is King)*, the king said it would scarcely ever get noticed; but in 1661 the Parliament noticed it and ordered that it be burned by the hangman at the cross of Edinburgh.

The godly assemby who produced the Westminster Confession succinctly expressed their belief about children who died in infancy: 'Elect infants, dying in infancy, are regenerated and saved by Christ through the Spirit, who works when, and where, and how he pleases.'[1]

While attending the Assembly in London, Rutherford lost two of his children. In fact, Rutherford was survived only by his second wife, Jean, and daughter, Agnes. His first wife and all their children, along with six children of his second marriage, predeceased him.

Rutherford is famous for his *Letters*, at least three of which he wrote to comfort bereaved parents. Rutherford's consolations to these mourners do not betray the theology expressed in the *Confession of Faith*. His words unite the precision of a theologian, the pastoral care of a minister, and the passion of a man who was himself a bereaved father. Tokens from each of Rutherford's three

---

[1] *Westminster Confession of Faith*, Chap. X. Princeton Theological Seminary professor A. A. Hodge wrote: 'The phrase "elect infants" is precise and fit for its purpose. It is not intended to suggest that there are any infants not elect, but simply to point out the facts—(1) that all infants are born under righteous condemnation; and (2) that no infant has any claim in itself to salvation; and hence (3) the salvation of each infant, precisely as the salvation of every adult, must have its absolute ground in the sovereign election of God. It is certainly revealed in Scripture that none, either adult or infant, is saved except on the ground of a sovereign election; that is, all salvation for the human race is pure grace. It is not positively revealed that all infants are elect, but we are left, for many reasons, to indulge a highly probable hope that such is the fact. [See A. A. Hodge, *The Confession of Faith, A Handbook of Christian Doctrine Expounding the Westminster Confession* (Edinburgh: Banner of Truth, 1958).] My father, Charles Hodge, at the close of his long life spent in defense of Calvinism, wrote on one of his conference papers, in trembling characters, a little while before he died, "I am fully persuaded that the vast majority of the human race will share in the beatitudes and glories of our Lord's redemption." Remember that all who die before complete moral agency have been given to Christ.' (See A. A. Hodge, *Evangelical Theology* [Edinburgh: Banner of Truth, 1976].)

letters, which span forty years of ministry (the last written just seven months before his death), are reproduced here for the reader's encouragement.

To a Christian Gentlewoman [23 April 1628]:

My love in Christ remembered to you. I was indeed sorrowful when I left you, especially since you were in such heaviness after your daughter's death; yet I am sure you know that the weightiest end of the cross of Christ that is laid upon you, lies on your strong Saviour. For Isaiah said that in all your afflictions He is afflicted (Is. 63:9). O blessed Saviour, who suffers with you! Your soul may be glad, even to walk in the fiery furnace, with the Son of Man, who is also the Son of God. Take courage. When you tire, he will bear both you and your burden (Ps. 55:22). In a little while you shall see the salvation of God.

Your lease on your daughter has run out; and you can no more quarrel against your great Superior for taking what He owns, than a poor tenant can complain when the landowner takes back his own land when the lease is expired. Do you think she is lost, when she is only sleeping in the bosom of the Almighty? If she were with a dear friend, your concern for her would be small, even though you would never see her again. Oh now, is she not with a dear friend, and gone higher, upon a certain hope that you shall see her again in the resurrection? Your daughter was a part of yourself; and, therefore, being as it were cut in half, you will be grieved. But you have to rejoice; though a part of you is on earth, a great part of you is glorified in heaven.

Follow her, but do not envy her; for indeed it is self-love that makes us mourn for them that die in the Lord. Why? Because we cannot mourn for them since they are happy; therefore, we mourn on our own private account. Be careful then, that in showing your affection in mourning for your daughter that you are not, out of self-affection, mourning for yourself.

Consider what the Lord is doing. Your daughter has been plucked out of the fire, and she rests from her labours. Your Lord is testing you by casting you in the fire. Go through all fires to your rest. And now remember, that the eye of God is upon the burning bush, and it is not consumed; and He is gladly content that such a weak woman as you should send Satan away frustrated. Honour God now, and shame the strong roaring lion, when you seem weakest.

Should you faint in the day of adversity? Recall the days of old! The Lord still lives; trust in Him. Faith is exceedingly charitable and believes no evil of God. The Lord has placed in the balance your submission to His will and your affection for your daughter. Which of the two will you choose? Be wise; and as I trust you love Christ better, pass by your daughter, and kiss the Son. Men lop the branches off their trees so they may grow up high and tall. The Lord has lopped your branch off by taking from you many children, so that you would grow upwards, setting your heart above, where Christ is at the right hand of the Father.

Prepare yourself; you are nearer your daughter this day than you were yesterday. Run your race with patience; let God have what belongs to Him. Do not ask Him for the daughter who has been taken from you, the daughter of faith; but ask Him for patience; and in patience possess your soul. Lift up your head; your redemption draws near.

Your affectionate and loving
friend in the Lord Jesus,
Samuel Rutherford[2]

Reverend David Dickson and
Dear Brother [28 May 1640]:

Your Lord may gather his roses whenever He pleases. The farmer cannot harvest when he pleases, as the Lord can do. You are taught to know and adore His sovereignty which He exercises over you, and which is made radiant with mercy. The child has only changed a bed in the garden, and is planted up higher, nearer the sun, where he shall thrive better than in this wasteland.

Grace be with you.
S. R.[3]

---

[2] Samuel Rutherford, *Letters of Samuel Rutherford* (Edinburgh: Banner of Truth, 1973), p. 34.
[3] Ibid.

Mistress Craig [4 August 1660]:

You have learned to know Christ in the furnace, where dross is consumed and shining faith must come forth. I heard of the death of your son, Thomas. I would like you to know that I saw some spiritual marks of the new-birth and hope of the resurrection in him when he was dying here in this distant city. The Lord wisely appointed, in His perfect and holy decree, that your son should die in a far country, like the dear patriarchs who died in Egypt, precious to the Lord, though they lacked burials (Ps. 79:3). Your safest course is to be silent and utter no repining and fretting thoughts of God.

Your precious youth is perfected and glorified. Had his sickness been drawn out a year and a day under your watchful gaze, it would have lengthened out your pain and grief into many portions, and every parcel would have been a little death. But now His Holy Majesty has brought you the news all at once, without dividing the grief into many portions. It was not just yesterday's thought, but a counsel of the Lord of old. The Lord has loosened your grip, though it was fastened so sure on your son. I hope that your heart will yield. It is not safe to be pulling against the omnipotent Lord. Let the pull go with Him, for He is strong; and say, 'Thy will be done on earth, as it is in heaven.'

His holy ways are to be adored; sometimes the

husband dies before the wife, and sometimes the son before the mother. So has the only wise God ordered things for your family. Your son has been sent before you and is not lost. In all things, then, give thanks. Do not meditate too much on the sad circumstances or that you are not able to weep over his grave because he died in a strange land. Remember, all countries on the earth are equally near to heaven. But, I know that it is easier to give counsel than to suffer. May the only wise Lord give us faith!

My wife is also wounded by your present condition, and she suffers with you.

Grace be with you
S. R.[4]

❦

John Howie, in his book *The Scots Worthies,* said that 'in all of Rutherford's writings he breathes the true spirit of religion; but in his admirable *Letters,* he seems to have outdone himself, as well as everybody else. These, it must be acknowledged by all who have any relish for true piety, contain sublime flights of devotion, and must ravish and edify every sober, serious, and understanding reader.'

> *What tongue, what pen, or skill of men*
> *Can famous Rutherford commend!*
> *His learning justly rais'd his fame,*

[4] Ibid.

True goodness did adorn his name.
He did converse with things above,
Acquainted with Immanuel's love.
Most orthodox he was and sound,
And many errors did confound.
For Zion's King, and Zion's cause,
And Scotland's covenanted laws,
Most constantly he did contend,
Until his time was at an end.
At last he won to full fruition
Of that which he had seen in vision.[5]

---

[5] John Howie, *The Scots Worthies* (Edinburgh: Banner of Truth, 1995).

It is not my design to exasperate your troubles, but to heal them; and for that purpose have I sent you these papers, which I hope may be of use both to you and many others in your condition, since they are the after-fruits of my own troubles; things that I have not commended to you from another hand, but which I have, in some measure, proved and tasted in my own trials.

JOHN FLAVEL

10

Weep Not

John Flavel was an English Puritan, a pastor, and a prolific writer. His best-known book today is The Mystery of Providence, a practical work dealing with how to understand God's providential dealings with us. His Introduction to the book begins with a verse of David from Psalm 57:2: 'I will cry out to God Most High, to God who performs all things for me.'

Flavel writes that the greatness of God is a glorious and unsearchable mystery and that the condescension of the Most High God to men and women is a profound mystery. When these attributes meet, as they do in Scripture, they make up a matchless mystery. 'Here we find', Flavel said, 'the Most High God performing all things for a poor distressed creature.'

Flavel knew firsthand what distress in this life was like. He lost his wife and only son. Then he understood what was in the heart of the psalmist—for he lived it. It was no longer just David's prayer, but his own intense and fervent cry: 'Be merciful to me, O God, be merciful to me! For my soul trusts in you; and in the shadow of your wings I will make my refuge, until these calamities have passed by' (*Psa.* 57:1).

Flavel found encouragement in the sovereignty of a wise Spirit setting the wheels in motion and governing all things with blessed and happy designs. 'Indeed', said Flavel, 'it would not be worthwhile to live in a world devoid of God and Providence.'

With his theology firmly fixed and the comfort of God experienced, Flavel turned to helping others by writing a book with the lengthy title *A Token for Mourners: or the Advice of Christ to a Distressed Mother, Bewailing the Death of Her Dear and Only Son*. The book opens with the following letter, dedicated to his beloved brother and sister, in which the author talks of his own similar grieving and the fruit born of his own troubles:

The double tie of nature and grace, beside the many endearing passages that for so many years have linked and glued our affections so intimately, cannot but beget a tender sympathy in me with you under all your troubles. They make me say of every affliction which befalls you, 'Half's mine.' I find it is with our affections as with the strings of musical instruments exactly set at the same height, if one is touched, the other trembles, though it be at some distance.

Our affections are one, and so in a great measure have been our afflictions also. You cannot forget that in the years lately past, the Almighty visited my house with the rod, and in one year cut off from it the root, and the branch, the tender mother, and the only son. I have felt the effects of those strokes. Surely I was like an ox unaccustomed to the yoke. Yes, I may say, 'Remembering mine affliction and my misery, the wormwood and the gall, my soul hath them still in remembrance, and is humbled in me' (*Lam.* 3:19-20). I dare not say that I ever felt my heart rising and swelling in discontentment against God; no, I could still justify Him, even when I most sensibly felt the sharp pain of His hand upon me. If He had plunged me into a sea of sorrow, yet I could say there is not a drop of injustice.

It was my earnest desire to visit you, as soon as I had strength and opportunity for so great a journey, so that, if the Lord had pleased, I might both refresh and be refreshed by you, after all my sad and disconsolate days. You cannot imagine what pleasure I had hoped would come from that visit; but it proved to us, as all other comforts of the same kind ordinarily do, more in expectation than in fruition.

For how soon after our joyful meeting and embraces did the Lord overcast and darken our day, by sending death into your home, to take away the desire of your eyes with a stroke! To crop off that sweet and only bud from which we promised ourselves so much comfort. But no more of that, I fear I have gone too far already. It is not my design to exasperate your troubles, but to heal them; and for that purpose have I sent you these papers, which I hope may be of use both to you and many others in your condition, since they are the after-fruits of my own troubles; things that I have not commended to you from another hand, but which I have, in some measure, proved and tasted in my own trials.

But I will not hold you longer here; I only have a few things to desire for, and from you, and then I am done. The things I desire are,

First, that you will not be too hasty to get off the yoke which God has put upon your neck. Remember when your child was in the womb, neither of you desired the infant to be delivered till God's appointed time was fully come. Now you travail again with sorrow for the baby's death. Do not desire to be delivered from your sorrows one moment before God's appointed time for your deliverance has fully come as well. Let patience have its perfect work. Comfort which comes in God's way and season will stick by you and do you good indeed.

Secondly, even though you and your afflictions had a sad meeting, I desire that you and they may have a comfortable parting. If they obtain God's blessing upon them in their work upon your hearts, surely they will have your blessing too at their valediction. And what you entertained with fear, you will dismiss with praise. How sweet is it to hear the afflicted soul say, when God is loosening His hands, 'It is good for me that I have been afflicted.'

Thirdly, I heartily wish that through these searching afflictions you may come to see more of the evil of sin, the emptiness of this world, and the fullness of Christ, than you ever saw before. Afflictions are searchers, and put the soul upon searching and trying its ways (*Lam.* 3:40). Happy are we, if by the light of affliction, we recognize our own sin. Blessed is the man whom God chastens and teaches His law (*Psa.* 94:12). There are unseen causes, many times, of our troubles; you have an advantage now to sift out the seeds and principles from which they spring.

Fourthly, I wish that all the love and delight you bestowed on your little one, may now be placed upon Jesus Christ; and that the stream of your affection to Him may be so much the stronger, as there are now fewer channels for it to be divided into. O deliver up all to Him, and say, 'Lord, take the whole heart entirely, and undivided to Thyself. Henceforth let there be no parting, sharing or dividing of the affections between God and the creature; let all the streams meet, and centre in Thee only.'

Fifthly, that you may be strengthened with all might in the inner man to all patience, that the peace of God may keep your hearts and minds, labour to bring your hearts to a meek submission to the rod of your Father. We had fathers of the flesh who corrected us, and we gave them reverence; shall we not much more be in subjection to the Father of spirits, and live? Is it right for children to contest and strive with their father? Or is it the way to be freed from the yoke by struggling under it? O that your hearts might be in a like frame with his that said, 'Lord, thou shalt beat, and I will bear.' It was a good observation that one made: 'The soul grows wise by sitting still and quiet under the rod.' And the apostle calls those excellent fruits which the saints gather from their sanctified afflictions, The peaceable fruits of righteousness (*Heb.* 12:11).

Lastly, my heart's desire and prayer to God for you, is, that by these frequent converses with death in your family, you may be prepared for your own change and dissolution, when it shall come.

O friends! how many graves have you and I seen opened for our dear relations? How often has death come up into your windows, and summoned the delight of your eyes? It is but a little while, and we shall go to them; we and they are distinguished but by short intervals.

Our dear parents are gone, our lovely and desirable children are gone, our bosom relations, that were as our own souls, are gone; and do not all these warning-knocks at our doors, acquaint us with the fact that we must prepare to follow shortly after them?

O that by these things our own death might be both more easy and familiar to us; the oftener it visits us, the better we should be acquainted with it; and the more of our beloved relations it removes before us, the less of either snare or entanglement remains for us when our turn comes.

My dear friends, my flesh and my blood, I beseech you, for religion's sake, for your own sake, and for my sake, whose comfort is in great part bound up in your prosperity and welfare, that you read frequently, and ponder seriously, and apply believingly these Scripture consolations and directions, which in some haste, I have gathered for your use; and the God of all consolation be with you.

I am,
Your most endeared Brother,
John Flavel[1]

In the book *A Token for Mourners,* Flavel draws out from the Gospel of Luke (7:13) the story of the bereaved mother who sought out the Master: 'When the Lord saw her, he had compassion on her and said to her, "Do not weep."' Flavel makes the point that angels are above the strokes of grief, but we are not. Animals sense no sorrow, but we do. This being true, to bear up under our sorrows is the wisdom, duty, and excellency of a Christian. To be parents to children is the firmest tie of affection. To bury a child must rip the heart of a parent. This was the condition of the woman in Luke 7. But Christ pitied her and told her not to weep, for He was about to raise her son from the dead!

Flavel remarked that this was an extraordinary, special resurrection; no parents that now carry their children to the grave may expect to receive them from the dead immediately. Yet, he concludes, if children die in Christ,

[1] John Flavel, *A Token for Mourners,* in *Works of John Flavel* (Edinburgh: Banner of Truth, 1982).

their parents come within the same reach of Christ's compassion and power. Weep not! The ground of all solid comfort and relief against the death of loved ones lies in the general and last resurrection. We shall see and enjoy them again at the Lord's coming (*1 Thess.* 4:17). Flavel believed this, and he spoke these things for the comfort of others.

THE CHILD'S FIRST GRIEF

Oh, call my brother back to me,
  I cannot play alone;
The summer comes, with flower and bee,
  Where is my brother gone?

The flowers run wild, the flowers we sowed
  Around our garden tree;
Our vine is dropping with its load—
  Oh, call him back to me.

He wouldn't hear thy voice, fair child,
  He may not come to thee;
His face that once like summer smiled,
  On earth no more thou'lt see.

A rose's brief, bright life of joy,
  Such unto him was given.
Go, thou must play alone, my boy,
  Thy brother is in Heaven.

And has he left his birds and flowers?
  And must I call in vain?
And through the long, long summer hours
  Will he not come again?

And by the brook, and in the glade,
  Are all our wanderings o'er?
Oh, while my brother with me played,
  Would I had loved him more.

FELICIA D. HEMANS[1]

[1] Felicia D. Hemans, in *The Girls' Book of Poetry: A Selection of Short Pieces, Lyrical, Descriptive, Pathetic and Narrative* (London: Ward, Lock & Co., 1883).

11

No More Crying:

A Token For Children

Adults can find comfort in reading accounts of godly parents with whom they share a common bond. But what about children who grieve for a brother or sister? What may we offer them? They, of course, have much in common with children of past ages. More often than today, those youngsters saw brothers, sisters, and playmates buried, and they were taught early to prepare for death. They memorized evening prayers such as:

> *Now I lay me down to sleep,*
> *I pray the Lord my soul to keep;*
> *if I should die before I wake,*
> *I pray the Lord my soul to take.*

Parents even read stories of the deaths of godly children to encourage their children to consider the eternal destiny of their own souls.[1]

Parents should teach their children the truths of our Christian faith. In times of grief, comfort them with words from the Bible:

---

[1] See the Puritan work by James Janeway, *A Token for Children* (Morgan, PA: Soli Deo Gloria Publications, 1994).

The Lord himself will descend from heaven with a shout, with the voice of an archangel, and with the trumpet of God. And the dead in Christ will rise first. Then we who are alive and remain shall be caught up together with them in the clouds to meet the Lord in the air. And thus we shall always be with the Lord.

1 THESSALONIANS 4:16-17

Teach your children that the Lord will return and live with his people in the heavenly city, and that city will be 'full of boys and girls playing in its streets' (*Zech.* 8:5).

When death comes to a family, a young child is unable to judge the true source of comfort; the parent must judge for him. If we do not have the right compass in such matters, we will not chart a wise and comforting course for our child; we will not 'train up a child in the way he should go' (*Prov.* 22:6). What we make of death is what they will make of it. So it comes back to us to seek our comfort in the Lord. There we shall find a fountain of hope and joy and peace, the springs of which will overflow from us to our children.

More than this, wise parents look for opportunities to teach their children valuable lessons. What better time to teach a child about life and death and the world to come than in the days and months following the death of a family member. We should be so zealous for our children's souls that we point them to real and lasting comfort in the Saviour. Instruct them in godliness and in the eternal blessings of those who die in Christ. Teach them this verse:

God will wipe away every tear from their eyes; there shall be no more death, nor sorrow, nor crying.

REVELATION 21:4

Then read them this story written by Bishop J. C. Ryle in the nineteenth century.

❧

Beloved children, I am going to tell you something which, I hope, will make you remember this verse as long as you live. I am going to tell you of three places about which the Bible says a great deal. It doesn't matter much what we know about some places; but it matters much to know something about these three places.

There is a place where there is a great deal of crying. What is this place? It is the world where you and I live. It is a world full of beautiful and pleasant things. The sun shining by day and the stars by night; the blue hills looking up to heaven, and the rolling sea ebbing and flowing; the broad quiet lakes, and the rushing restless rivers; the flowers blooming in the spring, and the fields full of corn in autumn; the birds singing in the woods, and the lambs playing in the meadows—all, all are beautiful things. I could look at them for hours and say, 'What a beautiful world it is!' But still it is a world where there is a great deal of crying. It is a world where there are many tears.

There was crying in Bible times. There is crying now

all over the world. Little babies cry when they want something or feel pain. Boys and girls cry when they are hurt, afraid or corrected by their parents. Grown -up people cry sometimes when they are in trouble, or when they see those die whom they love. Wherever there is sorrow and pain, there is crying.

You have seen people come to church all dressed in black. That is called being in mourning. Some family member or friend is dead, and therefore they dress in black. Well! remember when you see people in mourning, somebody has been crying. You have seen graves in churchyards, and have heard that when people die, they are buried there. Some of them are very little graves, not longer than you are. Well! remember that when those graves were made, and little coffins were let down into them, there was crying.

Children, did you ever think why there is all this crying? How it first began? Did you ever hear how weeping and tears came into the world? God did not make crying—that is certain. All that God made was 'very good'. Listen to me and I will tell how crying began.

Crying came into the world because of sin—it is the cause of all weeping, and tears, and sorrow, and pain upon the earth. All the crying began when Adam and Eve ate the forbidden fruit and became sinners. It was sin which brought pain and sickness and death into the world. Sin brought into the world selfishness, unkindness, arguing, stealing and fighting. If there had been no sin, there would have been no weeping; no sin, no crying. See now, my beloved children, how much you should hate sin. All the unhappiness in the world came from sin. How can anyone take pleasure in sin? Do not do that! Watch against sin. Fight with it. Avoid it and don't listen to it. Say to yourself every morning, 'Sin caused crying, and so I will hate sin.'

So, children, do not look for perfect happiness in this world; you will not find it. The world is a place where there is much crying and things do not always go pleasantly. I hear many boys and girls talking of pleasures they will have when they are men and women. I am sorry for them when I hear them talking this way. I know they are mistaken. I know they will be disappointed. They will find when they grow up, that they cannot get through the world without many troubles and cares. There are no roses without thorns. There are no years without dark and rainy days. There is no living on earth without crying and tears.

There is a place where there is nothing but crying. What is this place? It is the place where all bad people go when they are dead. The Bible calls this place hell. There is no laughter and smiling; there is nothing but weeping. There is no happiness. Those who go there cry night and day without stopping. They never go to sleep and wake up happy. They never stop crying in hell.

Beloved children, I am sorry to tell you that there are many people going to hell. It makes me sad to say these things, and I cannot bear the thought of boys and girls going to the dreadful place where there is nothing but crying. My heart's desire and prayer to God for you is, that you may not go there. So I want you to know some things which you must think about. Listen to my questions. Do you love Jesus Christ? You ought to love him. He died for your sins upon the cross that he might save you from hell. He died that your sins might be forgiven. Dear children, think about this! Be careful. If you do not love Christ you are not in the right way.

Do you try to please Christ? You ought to do this. In the Bible you may read that Jesus Christ said, 'If you love me, do what I command.' Think about this. If you are selfish or tell lies or fight with others, you are doing what he says not to do. Be careful so that you do not go to the place where there is only crying.

Do you say your prayers? You should do this. Ask God to take care of you and help you to obey. If you never pray, your heart will soon be full of mischief and sin. I once heard of a boy who was given a little garden full of flowers. But he did nothing for it. He never raked it or pulled out the weeds. After a few weeks there were many weeds, and the flowers died. Dear children, think about this and ask God to put his Holy Spirit in your hearts and protect you from the devil.

Do you read your Bible? You should do so. That beautiful book is able to save your soul and keep you from going to the place where there is nothing but crying. I once heard of a little boy in Africa who was sleeping with his father outdoors, near a fire. He awoke in the middle of the night and saw a great lion close to him.

The lion was about to pounce on him, but the little boy took a stick out of the fire and put it in the lion's face, and drove him away. Dear children, think about this! The devil is like a roaring lion. You must read your Bible if you would drive him away. If you do not read your Bible you will be in great danger.

There is a place where there is no crying at all. What is this place? It is heaven—the place where all good people go when they are dead. There all is joy and happiness. There are no tears. Sorrow and pain and sickness and death are not there. Nothing is there that will cause you any grief. Schools will be closed; there will be no more work. Heaven is an eternal rest for the people of God. There will be no more sickness in heaven. People who live there will not say 'I am sick.' They will always be well. There will only be strength and health forevermore. There will be no sin in heaven. There will be no bad tempers, no unkind words, no hateful actions. The devil will not be allowed to come in and spoil the happiness. There will be nothing but holiness and love forevermore.

Best of all, there can be no crying in heaven because the Lord Jesus Christ is there. Everyone who goes to heaven will see his face and be with him forever. He will take you in his arms and wipe away all tears from your eyes. With him there will be fullness of joy and pleasures forevermore.

Dear children, do you want to go to heaven? We cannot always live in this world. A day will come when we must die, like the old people who have died already. Children, would you like to go there when you die? Then listen to me, and I'll tell you the way you must go.

First, you must have your sins forgiven and your hearts made new and good. The only One who can do this for you is Jesus Christ. He can wash away your sins because he died for sinners. He can make your hearts new by putting the Holy Spirit in them. He is the Way and the Door into heaven. He has the keys in his hand. If you want to go to heaven, you must ask Jesus Christ to let you in. Pray and ask him to prepare a place for you in heaven, to put your name in his book of life, and to make you a Christian. Ask him to forgive all your sins and put his Spirit in your hearts. Ask him to give you grace to make you good while you are young, and good when you grow up, so that you might be safe while you live, and happy forever when you die. Children, Jesus will do all this if you will only ask him. He has done it for many other children already. Do not be afraid to ask him. He was very kind to children when he was on the earth; ask him to be kind to you. Say to him, 'Lord Jesus, save me.'

And now, children, I have told you of three places. I have told you of a place where there is nothing but crying. I hope you will not go there. I have told you of a place where there is no crying. I hope you will go there. I have told you of a place where there is a great deal of crying. That place is the world in which you are living. Now I will tell you the best way to be happy here.

The happiest people in this world are the ones who read the Bible often. They believe the Bible. They love Jesus Christ, and they try to obey what the Bible commands. No one is more happy than these people. They may become sick or go through troubles, but they are patient. They are happy because the Bible is their best friend. Children, remember my last words. The way to get through this world with the least possible crying is to read the Bible, believe the Bible, pray over the Bible, live by the Bible. If you go through life this way, you will have the least crying in this world. And best of all, you will have no crying at all in the world to come.[2]

I have no greater joy than to hear that my children are walking in the truth.

3 JOHN 4 (ESV)

And God will wipe away every tear from their eyes; there shall be no more death, nor sorrow, nor crying. There shall be no more pain, for the former things have passed away.

REVELATION 21:4

---

[2] J. C. Ryle, *No More Crying!* in *The Banner of Truth: Magazine Issues 1–16* (Edinburgh: Banner of Truth 2005), pp. 215–20.

Oh, troubled heart, be still and learn that no selfishness can be in love; that he who loves his Master withholds nothing when He has need of it; and he who loves his child will sink all sense of loss in the everlasting gain of lying safe upon the bosom of the Shepherd.

BENJAMIN M. PALMER

12

LESSONS IN SORROW

As we come to the end of this book, we have journeyed with many noble Christians as they walked the path from grief to glory. We have surveyed the road of their travels, beginning with the death and burial of a child, then down into the dark valley, and finally up again into a life of self-sacrifice for the glory of God and for the good of others. Here we stop for one last look at one of these travelers, a man by the name of Benjamin Morgan Palmer.

Rev. B. M. Palmer lived from 1818 to 1902. He was a compatriot of Robert Lewis Dabney, and like him, Palmer had a long and distinguished ministry in the church. He also buried five of his six children, and he left us a legacy—a book about his experiences entitled *The Broken Home: Lessons in Sorrow*. In his introductory note, Palmer writes:

> The 'stricken deer', says the poet Cowper, withdraws 'to seek a tranquil death in distant shades.' And so the mourner would like to hide his wound beneath his cloak. But the fraternal spirit of those in sorrow would pour the healing balm into other hearts which the Spirit of Consolation may have given to each. From the simple desire

of comforting those who mourn, this story of repeated bereavements is here told . . . Long-treasured memories are now scattered upon the winds, with the prayer that they may help to 'bind up the broken-hearted'.[1]

❀

In the opening chapter of the book, Palmer introduces us to his firstborn child. He recalls his thoughts as a new father, the joys of the few months of his son's life, the hopes he had for his boy, the ravages of disease in his son's body, and the first lesson he was taught by the sorrows of a child's death. Palmer wrote all this for our instruction and comfort.

❀

The morning was opening its eye in the first gray streak upon the horizon when a faint cry came from the upper room. Instantly, the hurried steps of one pacing uneasily to and fro in the hall beneath came to a stop. It was a cry which, when once heard, is never forgotten: the low, flat wail of a baby just entering into the world—the symbol of pain, warning beforehand of all it must suffer between the cradle and the grave.

The cry fell now, for the first time, upon ears which

---

[1] Benjamin M. Palmer, *The Broken Home, or, Lessons in Sorrow* (New Orleans: E. S. Upton, 1890).

had ached through the weary night to catch the sound. The long suspense was over. The young father bowed himself on the spot where he stood and poured out his heart in grateful praise to God.

Solemn thoughts crowd together in the first parental consciousness—thoughts that later deepen in significance, but never so startling as when they first rush upon the soul.

'Little miniature of myself. Claiming by equal right the ancestral name, and taking it from me when I am dead! Soon to be strong and tall as I—coming more into the foreground, and pushing me nearer to the edge over which I must topple in the end! Sole occupant then of all my estate; the mysterious link that binds me to the generations that follow, in whom all my earthly immortality reside. And yet, in all this formidable rivalry, I clasp this firstborn to my heart without the least bit of jealousy.'

With a proud joy the father tosses his firstborn into the air and catches him back screaming with delight, in utter unconsciousness of any peril. Are not these threads of childhood fun woven into the family life everywhere? And then the father with thoughtful pride bends over the sleeping babe and thinks of what he will someday become. Though life is short, is it not filled with repetitions? We scarcely begin to realize the hopes of our own youth, before we drop into the lives of our children in dreamy anticipation of their future.

So, during these twenty months, hopes were springing up in this young father's thoughts. Would the son take his father's mantle and become an ambassador of Christ? Ah, you who pray, you know the way in which the answer is returned? "We walk by faith, not by sight;" and a careful eye is needed to read the faithfulness of God in our bitter disappointments.

While in visions of the future, the young minister was casting his robe of office upon the child, an angel's wings touched the babe and dropped into its cradle the call to higher ministries beyond the stars. It was seen in the earthly decay which shriveled up the little form, until the loose flesh lapped over the thin bones like an ill-fitting garment. The hunger of disease could find nothing to satisfy its craving appetite but the body on which it fed; and the breathing skeleton lay finally upon a pillow on the mother's lap. How old the child grew in two short months. Every trace of infant beauty was effaced, only the golden curls floated over the pale brow; and the brilliant eyes which strangers in the street stooped to gaze upon, now burned with a feverish luster. Half closed in the uneasy sleep of sickness, even death could not seal them up. In his very coffin they peered out from beneath the soft lashes.

It is more than forty years since then, and the frost of winter has whitened the hair upon that father's head; but across the stretch of all those years, two hazel eyes, bright as coals of Juniper, still burn before his vision; and the memory is fresh as yesterday of the oldish look, coming out of eternity and resting upon that dying infant. Ah! who can tell how the two worlds may overlap at the border where they touch; or the way of the Free and Sovereign Spirit in His dealing with a soul standing at the gates of Heaven? The great mystery of death, how it swallows up the lesser mysteries of life which are so perplexing! Reader, in that narrow hour we shall touch them all; and the great revelation will come immediately after, in the light of the Throne.

For a time, hope and fear were kept evenly balanced in the scales. But, at length, the beam went down and fear deepened into anguish. As the grim certainty became more sure each day, there was again pacing back and forth; and solemn questions came up and shook the father's heart.

'This little soul which I had hoped to lead through knowledge to God, must I not lead it still in another way, seeing that He calls for him from above? O Savior, if this be Your voice saying as of old, 'of such is the kingdom of Heaven,' who am I that I should forbid it? If to be taken into Thine arms is to be blessed forever, then like the mothers who brought their children to Jesus, let me bring this little one to You, even in death, for the great benediction. Oh, troubled heart, be still and learn that no selfishness can be in love; that he who loves his Master withholds nothing when He has need of it; and he who loves his child will sink all sense of loss in the everlasting gain of lying safe upon the bosom of the Shepherd.'

And so the sharp struggle between nature and grace within the father was ended in the submission which said, 'not my will, but Thine, be done.' It was the first lesson that came out of sorrow.[2]

My Son! thou wast my heart's delight,
Thy morn of life was gay and cheery;
That morn has rushed to sudden night,
Thy father's house is sad and dreary.

I held thee on my knee, my Son,
And kissed thee laughing, kissed thee weeping;
But ah, thy little day is done,
Thou art with thy angel sister sleeping.

The staff on which my years should lean
Is broken, ere those years come o'er me;
My funeral rites thou shouldst have seen,
But thou art in the grave before me.

Thou rear'st to me no filial stone,
No parent's grave with tears beholdest;
Thou art my Ancestor, my Son,
And stand'st in Heaven's account the oldest.

On earth my lot was soonest cast,
Thy generation after mine;
Thou hast thy predecessor past—
Earlier Eternity is thine.

[2] Ibid.

I should have set before thine eyes
The road to Heaven, and showed it clear;
But thou untaught spring'st to the skies,
And leav'st thy teacher lingering here.

Sweet Seraph, I would learn of thee,
And hasten to partake thy bliss;
And oh, to thy world welcome me,
As first I welcomed thee to this.

Dear Angel, thou art safe in Heaven;
No prayers for thee need more be made;
Oh, let thy prayers for those be given
Who oft have blessed thy infant head.

My Father, I beheld thee born,
And led thy tottering steps with care;
Before me risen to Heaven's bright morn,
My Son, my Father, guide me there.

DANIEL WEBSTER[3]

Palmer closed the first chapter of his book with that poem by the American lawyer and statesman Daniel Webster, but not before giving the second lesson, solemn yet gracious, that came out of the first sorrow. This second lesson taught him what it meant to be a Christian father

[3] Ibid.

and to stand before God as the representative of his children. What good lessons! We, too, should learn them; first, to submit our wills to the supreme will and good pleasure of God; second, to stand before the Lord and be Christian parents to our sons and daughters.

Like so many others in this book, Benjamin Palmer's story does not end here, for he would be taught more lessons in grief. So he tells us:

Nineteen years bright with happiness and love chased far away the gloom of that first bereavement. Even the memory of it grew faint, as it shaded off in the distance; or when recalled, it was remembered without a pain because of the richness of the blessing that lay in it which had sanctified the years that came after. It was destined to be brought near again, by a relic which the grave would yield. Nineteen years of sunshine, and then the voice of weeping was heard again. Another grave must be dug, to receive the second born. She was laid to rest in a beautiful cemetery, upon the bank of a stream whose gentle flow murmured a soft and constant dirge over the sleepers by its side. 'Let the two lie together', said the parents as they wept, 'and we will carve upon the marble of the one "The little angel smiled and slept"; and upon the marble of the other, "She who, gentle as a saint, never gave us pain."'[4]

---

[4] Ibid.

The next lesson Palmer learned would be the greatest and most comforting. It is the lesson of the resurrection, which will conclude this book and the journey we have taken *from grief to glory*.

When blooming youth is snatched away
By death's resistless hand,
Our hearts the mournful tribute pay
Which pity must demand.

While pity prompts the rising sigh,
O, may this truth, impressed
With awful power, 'I, too, must die',
Sink deep in every breast.

Let this vain world engage no more;
Behold the opening tomb;
It bids us seize the present hour;
Tomorrow death may come.

O, let us fly—to Jesus fly;
Whose powerful arm can save;
Then shall our hopes ascend on high,
And triumph o'er the grave.

Great God, Thy sovereign grace impart,
With cleansing, healing power;
This only can prepare the heart
For death's surprising hour.

ANNE STEELE[1]

---

[1] Anne Steele, in *The Christian Hymn Book for the Sanctuary and Home* (Dayton, Ohio: Christian Publishing Association, 1875).

EPILOGUE
CONSIDER THE WORK OF GOD

God has revealed in his Word that all things work together for good, for the best, to those that love him, even to those that are called according to his purpose (*Rom.* 8:28). But, one may ask, how do I make sense of that truth in the death of a child, particularly a young child or infant?

First, we should pray and ask God to grant us wisdom, for 'he that handleth a matter wisely shall find good: and whoso trusteth in the LORD, happy is he' (*Prov.* 16:20 KJV). Wisdom and trust, not intellect and emotion, are necessary if one would find true comfort and peace in death. This was the assessment of Thomas Boston, an eighteenth-century Scottish minister who saw two of his five children laid in the churchyard:

> A correct view of afflictions is altogether necessary to a Christian demeanor under them; and that view is to be obtained only by faith, not by sense; for it is the light of the Word alone that represents them justly, discovering in them the work of God, and, consequently, designs becoming the Divine perfections. When these are perceived by the eye of faith, and duly considered, we have a just view of afflicting incidents, fitted to quell

the turbulent motions of corrupt affections under dismal outward appearances.[1]

We ought also to seek the good, not so much in things or events, but in him who is the fountain of all blessings. We should learn from a wise old Christian who wrote, 'Thou hast shown me that the glory of everything that is sanctified to do good is not seen in itself, but in the source of its sanctification.'

If we rightly apprehend God and the majesty of his perfections—that he is infinite, eternal, and unchangeable in his being, wisdom, power, holiness, justice, goodness, and truth—then, and only then, we will be satisfied that whatever comes to pass must work for the good of those who love him, though we do not necessarily know how it is so. Then we will come to know that whatever cross we have been called to bear has been divinely selected to accomplish God's good and perfect will for us. Our cross will change from something ugly and unbearable to that which is precious to us, a change that is beautifully described by a forgotten woman in a poem entitled 'The Changed Cross':

---

[1] Thomas Boston, *The Crook in the Lot, or The Sovereignty and Wisdom of God in the Afflictions of Men Displayed* (London: Silver Trumpet Publications, 1989).

It was a time of sadness, and my heart,
Although it knew and loved the better part,
Felt wearied with the conflict and the strife,
And all the needful discipline of life.

And while I thought on these, as given to me,
My trial-tests of faith and love to be,
It seemed as if I never could be sure
That faithful to the end I should endure.

And thus, no longer trusting to His might
Who says, 'We walk by faith and not by sight',
Doubting, and almost yielding to despair,
The thought arose, 'My cross I cannot bear.'

'Far heavier its weight must surely be
Than those of others which I daily see;
Oh! if I might another burden choose,
Methinks I should not fear my crown to lose.'

A solemn silence reigned on all around,
E'en Nature's voices uttered not a sound;
The evening shadows seemed of peace to tell,
And sleep upon my weary spirit fell.

A moment's pause,—and then a heavenly light
Beamed full upon my wondering, raptured sight;
Angels on silvery wings seemed everywhere,
And angels' music thrilled the balmy air.

Then One, more fair than all the rest to see,
One to whom all the others bowed the knee,
Came gently to me, as I trembling lay,
And, 'Follow me', he said, 'I am the Way.'

Then, speaking thus, he led me far above,
And there, beneath a canopy of love,
Crosses of divers shape and size were seen,
Larger and smaller than my own had been.

And one there was, most beauteous to behold,—
A little one, with jewels set in gold.
'Ah! this', methought, 'I can with comfort wear,
For it will be an easy one to bear.'

And so the little cross I quickly took,
But all at once my frame beneath it shook;
The sparkling jewels, fair were they to see,
But far too heavy was their weight for me.

'This may not be', I cried, and looked again,
To see if there was any here could ease my pain;
But, one by one, I passed them slowly by,
Till on a lovely one I cast my eye.

Fair flowers around its sculptured form entwined,
And grace and beauty seemed on it combined.
Wondering, I gazed,—and still I wondered more,
To think so many should have passed it o'er.

But oh! that form so beautiful to see
Soon made its hidden sorrows known to me;
Thorns lay beneath those flowers and colours fair;
Sorrowing, I said, 'This cross I may not bear.'

And so it was with each and all around,—
Not one to suit my need could there be found;
Weeping, I laid each heavy burden down,
As my Guide gently said, 'No cross,—no crown.'

At length to Him I raised my saddened heart;
He knew its sorrows, bade its doubts depart;
'Be not afraid', He said, 'but trust in Me;
My perfect love shall now be shown to thee.'

And then, with lightened eyes and willing feet,
Again, I turned, my earthly cross to meet;
With forward footsteps, turning not aside,
For fear some hidden evil might betide;

And there—in the prepared, appointed way,
Listening to hear, and ready to obey—
A cross I quickly found of plainest form,
With only words of love inscribed thereon.

With thankfulness I raised it from the rest,
And joyfully acknowledged it the best,—
The only one, of all the many there,
That I could feel was good for me to bear.

And, while I thus my chosen one confessed,
I saw a heavenly brightness on it rest;
And as I bent, my burden to sustain,
I recognized my own old cross again.

But oh! how different did it seem to be,
Now I had learned its preciousness to see!
No longer could I unbelieving say,
'Perhaps another is a better way.'

Ah, no! henceforth my own desire shall be,
That He who knows my best should choose for me;
And so, whate'er His love sees good to send,
I'll trust it's best,—because He knows the end.[2]

That is how we make sense of death and all other great losses. Trust and wait upon the Lord who knows the end and purpose of all things. So said King David: 'I would have lost heart, unless I had believed that I would see the goodness of the LORD in the land of the living. Wait on the LORD; be of good courage, and he shall strengthen your heart; wait, I say, on the LORD!' (*Psa.* 27:13-14).

Be like John Brown of Haddington, Scotland, and his wife, Janet, who knew well the grief attending the death of a child. 'Often had the angel of death visited their roof,

---

[2] William Cullen Bryant, ed., *The Family Library of Poem and Song* (New York: Fords, Howard, and Hulbert, 1880).

and had borne away six of their children in infancy.' Only two of their children survived to adulthood. Despite these unpleasant providences, Brown was able to write:

> Let us keep waiting on God in the way of His judgments; in patience possessing our souls; seeing the Lord's hand in all that we meet with; humbling ourselves under humbling providences; mourning, but never murmuring under His hand; and ever remarking how the minutest circumstances of our lives are directed by the overruling providence of God.[3]

❦

Be merciful to me, O God, be merciful to me! For my soul trusts in You; and in the shadow of Your wings I will make my refuge, until these calamities have passed by. I will cry out to God Most High, to God who performs all things for me.

PSALM 51:1-2

As Christian parents there is much comfort in having a good hope that our departed little ones are now with Jesus Christ. Our hope is all the more comforting because it is not merely sentimental or wishful thinking, but is grounded on the Bible and in the knowledge of a God who has made promises to us 'and our children' (*Acts*

---

[3] Robert Mackenzie, *John Brown of Haddington* (Edinburgh: Banner of Truth, 1964).

2:39). Our hope, then, moves toward an assurance of things unseen. Leave sentiments and superstition behind; press ahead to a sure hope in the God who saves his children. May we thereby be comforted, and for such grace may we gladly worship Christ, the King of kings and Lord of lords.

I close this book with the promised old story of a father and mother—Benjamin Palmer and his wife—who went to a beautiful cemetery to bury their teenage daughter 'upon the bank of a stream whose gentle flow murmured a soft and constant dirge over the sleepers by its side'. It was the very spot where nineteen years before they had buried an infant son and the place where they learned a lesson about the resurrection.

> And so the pick-axe and the shovel threw aside the earth, which for many years had pressed upon the bosom of the infant. Only a few bones and the little skull. No, wait a second; and with trembling hand the father clipped one little curl from which the luster had faded, but twining still around the hollow temple. He placed it on the palm of his hand, without a word, before the eye of the mother. With a smothered cry she fell upon his neck. 'It is our boy's; I see it as long ago, the soft lock that curled upon his temple.' 'Take it, Mother; it is to us the prophecy of the resurrection; the grave has not the power to destroy.' The old tears were wept again, but through them God made the rainbow to shine.[4]

[4] Benjamin M. Palmer, *The Broken Home, or, Lessons in Sorrow*.

Each time I read this story, I am reminded of the small lock of John Cameron's hair that we keep among our mementoes of his life, and I look forward to the resurrection yet to come. On that day the dead in Christ shall rise to behold the face of the Saviour whom they have loved; and I will be reunited with my son throughout eternity, never to part again. Such is the hope of all who die in Christ. 'May we all meet in heaven at last', preached Charles Spurgeon, 'and there we shall be happy forever.'

The old tears were wept again; but through them God made the rainbow to shine.

Thus says the LORD: *'I will return to Zion, and dwell in the midst of Jerusalem. Jerusalem shall be called the City of Truth . . . The streets of the city shall be full of boys and girls playing in its streets.'*

ZECHARIAH 8:3, 5

Almighty God, Father of mercies and giver of all comfort; Deal graciously, we pray Thee, with all those who mourn, that casting every care on Thee, they may know the consolation of Thy love; through Jesus Christ our Lord. Amen.

THE BOOK OF COMMON PRAYER (1928)

APPENDIX

FURTHER CONVERSATIONS
WITH GOD AND MEN

William Romaine wrote, 'In books I converse with men, in the Bible I converse with God.' Here are further conversations with God and men for the encouragement of bereaved parents.

> Why do we weep for departed friends or shake at death's alarm? They have gone away; they were not driven away. They resigned their spirits, they died at the commandment of the Lord. They would have willingly stayed; but they gladly went. They have gone away; but they have gone home; their bodies to their long, though not last, home in the dust; their spirits to a better home in their Father's house above. They will come again, come again to us. The Lord will bring their spirits with him when he comes from heaven the second time, for the complete salvation of all his chosen, and their bodies will come forth out of their graves to meet them, incorruptible, immortal, powerful, glorious, and all death-divided Christian friends shall meet to part no more.[1]

> JOHN BROWN

[1] John Brown, *Discourses and Sayings of Our Lord* (Edinburgh: Banner of Truth Trust, 1990).

To everything there is a season, a time for every purpose under heaven: a time to be born, and a time to die. Better to go to the house of mourning than to the house of feasting, for that is the end of all men; and the living take it to heart. Sorrow is better than laughter, for by a sad countenance the heart is made glad. Consider the work of God; for who can make straight what he has made crooked? In the day of prosperity be joyful, but in the day of adversity consider: surely God has appointed the one as well as the other.

SELECTIONS FROM ECCLESIASTES

Around the throne of God in heav'n,
Thousands of children stand,
Children whose sins are all forgiv'n,
A holy, happy band,
Singing, 'Glory, glory, glory be to God on high.'

In flowing robes of spotless white
See ev'ry one arrayed;
Dwelling in everlasting light
And joys that never fade,
Singing, 'Glory, glory, glory be to God on high.'

What brought them to that world above,
That heav'n so bright and fair,

Where all is peace, and joy, and love;
How came those children there?
Singing, 'Glory, glory, glory be to God on high.'

Because the Savior shed his blood
To wash away their sin;
Bathed in that pure and precious flood,
Behold them white and clean,
Singing, 'Glory, glory, glory be to God on high.'

On earth they sought the Savior's grace,
On earth they loved his Name;
So now they see his blessed face,
And stand before the Lamb,
Singing, 'Glory, glory, glory be to God on high.'[2]

ANNE H. SHEPHERD

❦

Let the little children come to me, and do not forbid
them; for of such is the kingdom of God. Assuredly, I
say to you, whoever does not receive the kingdom of
God as a little child will by no means enter it.' And he
took them up in his arms, laid his hands on them, and
blessed them.

MARK 10:14-16

[2] Anne H. Shepherd, in *Trinity Hymnal* (Philadelphia: Great Commission Publications, 1961).

Clearly, accomplishment in life cannot be measured in terms of years alone. It often happens that those that die young have accomplished more than others who live to old age. Even infants, who sometimes have been with their parents only a few days, or even hours, may leave profound influences that change the entire course of the life of the family. And undoubtedly, from the Divine viewpoint, the specific purpose for which they were sent into the world was accomplished. It is our right neither to take life prematurely, nor to insist on its extension beyond the mark that God has set for it.[3]

LORAINE BOETTNER

It gives me great pleasure in a public and solemn manner to record my testimony for the glory of God, and the comfort of all his people, who may peruse these pages. It is this: that the tenderness of Christ to his sick and dying servants is great, and that in the hour of their last trial, he does not leave them, nor forsake them.

For a long time I have visited, as I had opportunity, the sick and suffering people of God, without regard

[3] Loraine Boettner, *Immortality* (Philadelphia: Presbyterian and Reformed Publishing, 1975).

to age, sex, rank, complexion, or denomination. Some left the world in a state of unconsciousness, but their last moments of rationality were cheered by blessed rays of light from heaven. Early in their sickness some were sorely tempted, but the victory came at last. Some had been subject to mental derangement, but they were permitted to enter eternity without a cloud over their reason. Yet had they died while still mentally ill, the promises of God would not have failed.

Some were young in years, and in Christian experience; but the good Shepherd gathered them like lambs in his arms, and carried them in his bosom. Some were in middle life, and left hopeless children behind them; but I have seen the dying mother kiss her little babe, and bid the world farewell with entire composure. The peace of God ruled her heart by Jesus Christ. Some were old, nervous, and, on other subjects, full of fancies; but Christ, the Rock, followed them to Canaan.

What God has done for his people in days past should encourage those who live at the present time. God's faithfulness to the departed should invigorate the faith and expel the fears of the waiting. God's people have left the world in various ways. Some have died violent and ignominious deaths, and some have died in their beds. Some have had long notice, and others hardly any. Some have died old, some in the midst of their days, and some in the morning of existence; yet they have all left an encouraging testimony to the power of Christ's grace to their departing spirits.

The great advantages of good examples are that they express with clearness the duty to be done, that they show the possibility of doing it, and that they incite us to imitation. These advantages are fully realized in the examples of dying saints.[4]

WILLIAM S. PLUMER, D.D.

Precious in the sight of the LORD *is the death of his saints.*

PSALM 116:15

When sickness, pain, and death
Come o'er a godly child,
How sweetly, then, departs the breath!
The dying pang, how mild!

It gently sinks to rest,
As once it used to do
Upon the tender mother's breast,
And as securely too.

---

[4] William S. Plumer, *The Grace of Christ, or Sinners Saved by Unmerited Kindness* (Harrisonburg, PA: Sprinkle Publications, 1997).

The spirit is not dead,
Though low the body lies;
But, freed from sin and sorrow, fled
To dwell beyond the skies.

That death is but a sleep
Beneath a Savior's care;
And He will surely safely keep
The body resting there.[5]

UNKNOWN

Let us consider, beloved brethren, that we are passing our time here as strangers and pilgrims. We embrace the day which assigns each to his home, which restores to Paradise and a kingdom, us who have been plucked from the world and set free from worldly snares. Who would not hasten home? Paradise we count our father-land, and the patriarchs our fathers. Why should we not hasten homeward to salute our parents? There the mighty multitude of dear ones awaits us—the crowd of parents, brothers, sons long for us, already secure of their own safety, and now concerned about ours.

[5] Taken from *The Psalms and Hymns, with Doctrinal Standards and Liturgy of the Reformed Church in America* (New York: Board of Publication of the R. P. Dutch Church in North America, 1859).

How great the joy to us and to them of beholding and embracing each other![6]

CYPRIAN

O merciful Father, whose face the angels of Thy little ones do always behold in heaven; Grant us steadfastly to believe that this Thy child hath been taken into the safe keeping of Thine eternal love; through Jesus Christ our Lord. Amen.

THE BOOK OF COMMON PRAYER (1928)

Calm on the bosom of thy God,
Young spirit, rest thee now;
E'en while with us thy footsteps trod,
His seal was on thy brow.
Dust to its narrow house beneath;
Soul to its place on high;
They that have seen thy look in death
No more may fear to die.
Lone are the paths, and sad the bowers,
Whence thy meek smile is gone;

[6] Quoted in Horatius Bonar, comp., *Words Old and New: Gems from the Christian Authorship of All Ages* (Edinburgh: Banner of Truth, 1994).

But O, a brighter home than ours,
In heaven, is now thine own.[7]

FELICIA D. HEMANS

❧

Mourn not ye, whose child hath found
Purer skies and holier ground;
Flowers of bright and pleasant hue,
Free from thorns, and fresh with dew.
Mourn not ye, whose child hath fled
From this region of the dead,
To yon winged angel-band,
To a better, fairer land.
Knowledge in that clime doth grow
Free from weeds of toil and woe,
Joys which mortals may not share;
Mourn ye not, your child is there.[8]

LYDIA H. SIGOURNEY

❧

---

[7] Felicia D. Hemans, in *The Christian Hymn Book for the Sanctuary and Home* (Dayton, Ohio: Christian Publishing Association, 1875).
[8] Lydia H. Sigourney, in *The Psalms and Hymns, with Doctrinal Standards.*

O God, whose most dear Son did take little children into His arms and bless them; Give us grace, we beseech Thee, to entrust the soul of this child to Thy never failing care and love, and bring us all to thy heavenly kingdom; through Thy Son, Jesus Christ our Lord. Amen.

THE BOOK OF COMMON PRAYER (1928)

Go to thy rest, fair child,
Go to thy dreamless bed,
While yet so gentle, undefiled,
With blessings on thy head.
Fresh roses in thy hand,
Buds on thy pillow laid,
Haste from this blighting land,
Where flow'rs so quickly fade.

Before thy heart could learn
In waywardness to stray;
Before thy feet could turn
The dark and downward way;
Ere sin had seared the breast,
Or sorrow woke the tear,
Rise to thy throne of changeless rest
In yon celestial sphere.

Because thy smile was fair,
Thy lip and eye so bright,
Because thy loving cradle-care
Was such a dear delight;
Shall love, with weak embrace
Thy upward wing detain?
No, gentle angel; seek thy place
Amid the cherub train.[9]

LYDIA H. SIGOURNEY

Fare thee well, thou fondly cherished;
Dear, dear spirit, fare thee well.
He who sent thee now hath called thee
Back with Him and His to dwell.

Like a sunbeam through our dwelling
Shone thy presence, bright and calm;
Thou didst add a zest to pleasure;
To our sorrows thou wast balm.

Yet while mourning, O, our lost one,
Come no visions of despair;
Seated on thy tomb, Faith's angel
Saith, Thou art not, art not there.

[9] Lydia H. Sigourney, in *Hymn Book of the Methodist Episcopal Church, South* (Nashville, Tenn.: Publishing House of the M. E. Church, South, 1889).

Where, then, art thou? With the Saviour,
Blest, forever blest, to be;
'Mid the sinless little children
Who have heard this: 'Come to me.'

Passed the shades of death's dark valley,
Thou art leaning on His breast,
Where the wicked may not enter
And the weary are at rest.[10]

DAVID MACBETH MOIR

&

Ye mourning saints, whose streaming tears
Flow o'er your children dead;
Say not, in transports of despair,
That all your hopes are fled.

If, cleaving to that darling dust,
In fond distress ye lie,
Rise, and with joy and reverence view
A heavenly parent nigh.

Though, your young branches torn away,
Like withered trunks ye stand,
With fairer verdure shall ye bloom,

---

[10] David MacBeth Moir, in *The Christian Hymn Book for the Sanctuary and Home* (Dayton, Ohio: Christian Publishing Association, 1875).

'I'll give the mourner', saith the Lord,
'In My own house a place';
No names of daughters nor of sons
Could yield so high a grace.

Transient and vain is every hope
A rising race can give;
In endless honour and delight
My children all shall live.

We welcome, Lord, those rising tears,
Through which Thy face we see;
And bless those wounds, which through our hearts
Prepare a way for Thee.[11]

PHILIP DODDRIDGE

🙰

When peace, like a river, attendeth my way,
When sorrows like sea billows roll;
Whatever my lot, thou hast taught me to say,
It is well with my soul.

Though Satan should buffet, though trials should come,
Let this blest assurance control;
That Christ has regarded my helpless estate,
And has shed his own blood for my soul.

---

[11] Philip Doddridge, in *The Psalms and Hymns, with Doctrinal Standards.*

My sin—O the bliss of this glorious thought!—
My sin, not in part, but the whole,
Is nailed to the cross and I bear it no more;
Praise the Lord, praise the Lord, O my soul!

O Lord, haste the day when the faith shall be sight,
The clouds be rolled back as a scroll,
The trump shall resound and the Lord shall descend;
'Even so'—it is well with my soul.

It is well with my soul;
It is well, it is well with my soul.[12]

Horatio G. Spafford

[12] Horatio G. Spafford, in *Trinity Hymnal*. Spafford's wife and children were sailing to England when their ship sank. His wife was rescued, but all their children were lost at sea. Spafford later wrote this hymn near the place where they perished.

SELECT BIBLIOGRAPHY

Anyabwile, Thabiti M., *The Faithful Preacher: Recapturing The Vision Of Three Pioneering African-American Pastors* (Wheaton: Crossway Books, 2007).

Bennett, Arthur, ed., *The Valley of Vision, A Collection of Puritan Prayers and Devotions* (Edinburgh: Banner of Truth, 1997).

Blumhofer, Edith L., *Her Heart Can See: The Life and Hymns of Fanny J. Crosby* (Grand Rapids: Eerdmans, 2005).

Boettner, Loraine, *Immortality* (Philadelphia: Presbyterian and Reformed Publishing, 1975).

Bonar, Horatius, comp. *Words Old and New: Gems from the Christian Authorship of All Ages* (Edinburgh: Banner of Truth, 1994).

Boston, Thomas, *The Crook in the Lot, or The Sovereignty and Wisdom of God in the Afflictions of Men Displayed* (London: Silver Trumpet Publications, 1989).

Bryant, William Cullen, ed., *The Family Library of Poem and Song* (New York: Fords, Howard, and Hulbert, 1880).

Bunyan, John, *Works of John Bunyan* (Edinburgh: Banner of Truth, 1991).

Calvin, John, *Letters of John Calvin* (Edinburgh: Banner of Truth, 1980).

Cooley, Timothy M., *Sketches of the Life and Character of the Rev. Lemuel Haynes* (Harper & Brothers, 1837; repr. New York: Negro Universities Press, 1969).

Cook, Faith, *Selina, Countess of Huntingdon* (Edinburgh: Banner of Truth, 2001).

Dallimore, Arnold A., *A Heart Set Free: The Life of Charles Wesley.* (Wheaton, IL: Crossway Books, 1988).

_____ *George Whitefield: The Life and Times of the Great Evangelist of the 18th Century Revival*, Vol. 2. (Edinburgh: Banner of Truth, 1995).

Demaus, Robert, *Hugh Latimer, A Biography* (London: The Religious Tract Society, 1903).

Douglass, Frederick, *My Bondage and My Freedom* (New York: Penguin Classics, 1855, repr. 2003).

_____ *Life and Times of Frederick Douglass, Written by Himself* (1882. The Online Library of Liberty at oll.libertyfund.org).

Edwards, Jonathan, *Works of Jonathan Edwards*, 2 Vols. (Edinburgh: Banner of Truth, repr. 1974).

Flavel, John, *Works of John Flavel* (Edinburgh: Banner of Truth, 1982).

Ford, Sallie R., *Mary Bunyan, The Dreamer's Blind Daughter: A Tale of Religious Persecution* (New York: Sheldon & Company, 1860; repr. Swengel: Reiner Publications, 1976).

Henry, Matthew, *Commentary on the Whole Bible* (McLean, VA: MacDonald Publishing Company, n.d.).

Johnson, Thomas Cary, *The Life and Letters of Robert Lewis Dabney* (Edinburgh: Banner of Truth, 1977).

Kieran, John, ed., *Poems I Remember* (Garden City, N.Y.: Garden City Publishing, 1945).

Kuyper, Abraham, *To Be Near Unto God* Trans. J. H. De Vries, (New York: Macmillan, 1918).

Mackenzie Robert, *John Brown of Haddington* (Edinburgh: Banner of Truth, 1964).

Manschreck, Clyde L., *Melanchthon: The Quiet Reformer,* (New York: Abingdon Press, 1958).

McFeely, William S., *Frederick Douglass* (New York: W. W. Norton & Company, 1991).

Murray, Iain H., *Jonathan Edwards, A New Biography* (Edinburgh: Banner of Truth, 1987).

Owen, John, *Works of John Owen,* Vol. 1 (London: Banner of Truth, 1965).

Pierson, A. T., *George Müller of Bristol and His Witness to a Prayer-Hearing God* (Old Tappan, NJ: Fleming H. Revell Company).

Romaine, William, *The Life, Walk, and Triumph of Faith* (London: Charles J. Thynne, n.d.).

Rutherford, Samuel, *Letters of Samuel Rutherford* (Edinburgh: Banner of Truth, 1973).

Ryle, J. C., 'Two Sermons for Children', *The Banner of Truth: Magazine Issues 1-16* (Edinburgh: Banner of Truth, 2005).

Smith, Preserved, ed., *The Life and Letters of Martin Luther,* (London: J. Murray, 1911).

Spurgeon, C. H. *Autobiography, Vol. 1: The Early Years*, (Edinburgh: Banner of Truth, 1985).

_____ *Letters of Charles Haddon Spurgeon* (Edinburgh: Banner of Truth, 1992).

Steer, Roger, ed., *Spiritual Secrets of George Müller*, (Wheaton, IL: Harold Shaw Publishers, 1985).

Tyerman, Luke, *The Life and Times of the Reverend George Whitefield*, Vol. 2. London: Hodder and Stoughton, 1877).

Warfield, B. B., *The Person and Work of Christ* (Philadelphia: Presbyterian and Reformed Publishing, 1950).

Whitefield, George, *Journals* (Edinburgh: Banner of Truth, 1989).

_____ *Letters* (Edinburgh: Banner of Truth, 1976).

For more information and resources
on parental grief and comfort, visit
www.grieftoglory.com